Blockchain Quick Start Guide

A beginner's guide to developing enterprise-grade decentralized applications

Xun (Brian) Wu
Weimin Sun

BIRMINGHAM - MUMBAI

Blockchain Quick Start Guide

Commissioning Editor: Amey Varangaonkar
Acquisition Editor: Reshma Raman
Content Development Editor: Mohammed Yusuf Imaratwale
Technical Editor: Jinesh Topiwala
Copy Editor: Safis Editing
Project Coordinator: Kinjal Bari
Proofreader: Safis Editing
Indexer: Mariammal Chettiyar
Graphics: Alishon Mendonsa
Production Coordinator : Deepika Naik

First published: December 2018

Production reference: 1241218

Published by Packt Publishing Ltd.
Livery Place
35 Livery Street
Birmingham
B3 2PB, UK.

ISBN 978-1-78980-797-4

`www.packtpub.com`

Contributors

About the authors

Xun (Brian) Wu is an author, founder, and advisor. He has over 17 years of extensive hands-on experience in the design and development of blockchain, big data, cloud, UI, and system infrastructure. He has worked for top investment banks including JP. Morgan, Citigroup, and the Bank of America. He is the co-author of *Seven NoSQL Databases in a Week*, *Hyperledger Cookbook*, and *Blockchain By Example*, published by Packt. He has been a technical reviewer for more than 50 computer technical books for Packt Publishing. He serves as a board advisor for several blockchain start-ups. He owns several patents on blockchain. Brian holds a master's degree in computer science from NJIT. He lives in New Jersey with his two beautiful daughters, Bridget and Charlotte.

> *I would like to thank my parents, wife, and kids for their patience and support throughout this endeavor. I'd also like to thank Jianmin Liu, Ryan, and the many others who provided help and inspiration along the way.*

Weimin Sun has 20 years of experience of working in the financial industry. He has worked for top-tier investment and commercial banks such as J.P. Morgan, Bank of America, Citibank, and Morgan Stanley. He has managed large teams developing IT applications. He has held corporate titles such as Executive Director and Senior VP. He has in-depth knowledge of blockchain technology, data architecture, data modeling, data science, and big data platforms. He is an expert in designing data-driven solutions. He has a Ph.D, an M.B.A, and an M.Sc. He has published several papers on statistics in renowned academic journals. Weimin lives in New Jersey, USA, with his beautiful wife and his talented son.

> *I would like to thank my wife and son for their lasting support and love. I express my gratitude and appreciation to Ryan Duan for proofreading the entire book and helping to improve the book's quality greatly. I want to thank Professor Yang, Yixian for permitting me to use his idea of making the genealogy analogy to describe blockchain.*

About the reviewers

Aasim Ali is a full-stack blockchain engineer at Inncretech LLC, Princeton, New Jersey. He has a master's degree in information systems with a graduate certification in business intelligence from Stevens Institute of Technology, Hoboken, New Jersey. He works with the blockchain and data science R&D team making POCs around AI, Ethereum, and Hyperledger for clients to incorporate in their proprietary systems, which helps them upgrade to new cutting-edge technologies.

> *I would like to thank my family and friends for supporting me through my journey of life, which helped me grow into a knowledgeable and intellectual person. I would also like to express my special gratitude to my company's co-founder and CTO for believing in me and giving me this opportunity to explore blockchain in depth. I would sincerely like to thank the author and his team for giving me the opportunity to review this book.*

F. Richard Yu is the chair of the IEEE P2418.3/4 blockchain standards, IEEE fellow, IET fellow, and professor at Carleton University, Canada. He is the leading general co-chair of IEEE conference on blockchain, 2019. Professor Yu has published 6 books and over 490 papers in international top-tier academic journals and conferences, with over 13,000 citations and an H-index of 63. He holds 27 international patents, and his innovative works have been incorporated into industry standards, impacting on millions of pieces of network equipment and billions of mobile devices. He received his PhD from the University of British Columbia (UBC) in 2003.

Packt is searching for authors like you

If you're interested in becoming an author for Packt, please visit `authors.packtpub.com` and apply today. We have worked with thousands of developers and tech professionals, just like you, to help them share their insight with the global tech community. You can make a general application, apply for a specific hot topic that we are recruiting an author for, or submit your own idea.

Table of Contents

Preface

Just as we were at the dawn of the internet age in the nineties, we are at the dawn of the blockchain age now. This new technology will disrupt existing business models and give birth to new ones. It will inspire the emergence of community economies built on blockchain networks, where every participant makes contributions to and receives benefits from the community. There will no longer be a single entity controlling and receiving dividends from the economy.

Thanks to its immutability, transparency, and the consensus mechanism for avoiding double-spending, along with other clever designs such as blocks chained with the hashes of the previous blocks, the technology allows untrusting parties to trade with each other directly. As a result, most of the intermediary services currently provided by existing institutions will no longer be needed. As a consequence, blockchain technology is receiving attention the world over.

There are many articles and books on blockchain. However, there are no good books serving beginners who are looking for a quick way to gain a good understanding of the technology as a whole and learn what's needed to be able to develop a complete blockchain application. This quick guide fills in this gap. The book covers coding details on how to develop blockchain applications on Ethereum and Hyperledger Fabric, the two most popular platforms for public and enterprise blockchain, respectively.

Who this book is for

This book benefits readers who are new to the blockchain technology and want to learn about its basics and jump start their development of smart contracts and **Decentralized Applications** (**DApps**). Business readers can especially gain from the first two chapters along with the last chapter, which cover what business issues need to be addressed and what possible use cases there are for blockchain. IT readers should read all the chapters and learn how to develop smart contracts and DApps via the many working examples presented in this book.

What this book covers

`Chapter 1`, *Introduction to Blockchain Technology*, gives an overview of blockchain and its key concepts, such as cryptography and hash algorithms, the distributed ledger, transactions, blocks, proof of work, mining, and consensus. We cover Bitcoin, the mother of blockchain technology, in detail. We briefly introduce Ethereum by pointing out some limitations of Bitcoin and how they are addressed by Ethereum. While Bitcoin and Ethereum are examples of public blockchains, IBM's Hyperledger is used as an example of enterprise blockchains. Toward the end of this chapter, we look at the evolution of blockchain, through 1.0, 2.0, 3.0, and beyond, and we examine their use cases.

`Chapter 2`, *Ethereum Fundamentals*, covers the basic concepts of Ethereum, such as smart contracts, ether, consensus algorithms, EVM, gas, and accounts. We will discuss Ethereum performance and review ideas on how to improve the overall performance via proof of work, casper, plasma, and sharding.

`Chapter 3`, *Overview of Solidity Programming*, discusses what solidity is, as well as the tools for the solidity development environment. We then discuss smart contracts and their common patterns. We cover the important topic of smart contract security. Finally, we show how to write a smart contract with a use case of crowdfunding.

`Chapter 4`, *Building an Ethereum Blockchain Application*, looks at what a DApp is. We give a quick overview of web3.js. We explain how to set up an Ethereum development environment, as well as how to develop and test a DApp.

`Chapter 5`, *Exploring an Enterprise Blockchain Application Using Hyperledger Fabric*, gets into the key concepts of Hyperledger Fabric, along with the core components. We explain how to create a Hyperledger Fabric environment, how to write a chaincode, and how to set up Hyperledger Fabric configuration.

`Chapter 6`, *Implementing a Business Network Using Hyperledger Composer*, provides an overview of Hyperledger Composer and talks about how to set up a Hyperledger Composer environment. We discuss business scenarios, the business network archive, and how to implement a business transaction function.

`Chapter 7`, *Blockchain Use Cases*, first talks about popular blockchain use cases across industries, including the financial sector, civil services, supply chains, the **Internet of Things** (**IoT**), and healthcare, at a high level. We will then proceed to a discussion of the proper use cases for DApps, before then developing a successful DApp. Finally, we take the health data-sharing use case and comment at a high level on building an DApp for it.

To get the most out of this book

We've focused on organizing the book to fit business and IT beginners in blockchain technology. The chapters are arranged to ensure that they can be followed easily and flow naturally.

Business users can skip the chapters with detailed descriptions on how to develop blockchain applications and, instead, focus on the chapters with general descriptions of the technology and use cases.

Veteran IT professionals on blockchain can skip the general description chapters and focus on chapters either on Ethereum or Hyperledger, from which they will gain insights on how to build blockchain applications.

It is recommended that IT users download the code and make modifications for adopting to their own use cases or exercises.

Download the example code files

You can download the example code files for this book from your account at `www.packt.com`. If you purchased this book elsewhere, you can visit `www.packt.com/support` and register to have the files emailed directly to you.

You can download the code files by following these steps:

1. Log in or register at `www.packt.com`.
2. Select the **SUPPORT** tab.
3. Click on **Code Downloads & Errata**.
4. Enter the name of the book in the **Search** box and follow the onscreen instructions.

Once the file is downloaded, please make sure that you unzip or extract the folder using the latest version of:

- WinRAR/7-Zip for Windows
- Zipeg/iZip/UnRarX for Mac
- 7-Zip/PeaZip for Linux

The code bundle for the book is also hosted on GitHub at `https://github.com/PacktPublishing/Blockchain-Quick-Start-Guide`. In case there's an update to the code, it will be updated on the existing GitHub repository.

We also have other code bundles from our rich catalog of books and videos available at `https://github.com/PacktPublishing/`. Check them out!

Conventions used

There are a number of text conventions used throughout this book.

`CodeInText`: Indicates code words in text, database table names, folder names, filenames, file extensions, pathnames, dummy URLs, user input, and Twitter handles. Here is an example: "One important interface is `ChaincodeStubInterface`, which provides functions that allow you to query, update, and delete assets in the ledger."

A block of code is set as follows:

```
contract SimpleStorage {
    uint storedData; // State variable
    //...
}
```

When we wish to draw your attention to a particular part of a code block, the relevant lines or items are set in bold:

```
pragma solidity ^0.4.15;
import 'zeppelin/contracts/math/SafeMath.sol';
....
contract ExampleCoin is ERC20 {
  //SafeMath symbol is from imported file SafeMath.sol'
  using SafeMath for uint256;
   ...
}
```

Any command-line input or output is written as follows:

```
mkdir ~/insurance-claim && cd ~/insurance-claim
```

Bold: Indicates a new term, an important word, or words that you see onscreen. For example, words in menus or dialog boxes appear in the text like this. Here is an example: "When the preceding request is validated by mining nodes, the **HelloWorld** smart contract is invoked."

Warnings or important notes appear like this.

Tips and tricks appear like this.

Get in touch

Feedback from our readers is always welcome.

General feedback: If you have questions about any aspect of this book, mention the book title in the subject of your message and email us at `customercare@packtpub.com`.

Errata: Although we have taken every care to ensure the accuracy of our content, mistakes do happen. If you have found a mistake in this book, we would be grateful if you would report this to us. Please visit `www.packt.com/submit-errata`, selecting your book, clicking on the Errata Submission Form link, and entering the details.

Piracy: If you come across any illegal copies of our works in any form on the Internet, we would be grateful if you would provide us with the location address or website name. Please contact us at `copyright@packt.com` with a link to the material.

If you are interested in becoming an author: If there is a topic that you have expertise in and you are interested in either writing or contributing to a book, please visit `authors.packtpub.com`.

Reviews

Please leave a review. Once you have read and used this book, why not leave a review on the site that you purchased it from? Potential readers can then see and use your unbiased opinion to make purchase decisions, we at Packt can understand what you think about our products, and our authors can see your feedback on their book. Thank you!

For more information about Packt, please visit `packt.com`.

1
Introduction to Blockchain Technology

Blockchain technology will disrupt current business models by making intermediary services obsolete. The term *blockchain* has become a buzzword worldwide. IT technologists are picking up blockchain books in flocks and starting to read about it in the hope of mastering the basic concepts. People are motivated to become professional blockchain application developers. Unless you pick up a well-written book, it often requires you to read many books and articles before the concepts of the blockchain become clear. To assist you in gaining a concise view of how an end-to-end blockchain application works, we outline a high-level introduction of the basic concepts along with the code-level details explaining how an actual application can be developed step by step. At the end of this book, we cover blockchain use cases in examples to inspire you to work on life-changing projects.

In this chapter, we give an overview of blockchain, along with its key concepts such as cryptography and hash algorithms, the distributed ledger, transactions, blocks, proof of work, mining, and consensus. We cover Bitcoin, the mother of blockchain technology, in detail. We briefly introduce Ethereum by pointing out some limitations of Bitcoin and how they are addressed by Ethereum. While Bitcoin and Ethereum are examples of public blockchains, IBM's Hyperledger is used as an example of enterprise blockchains. At the end of this chapter, we mention the evolution of the blockchain: blockchain 1.0, 2.0, 3.0, and beyond, based on their use cases. Specifically, we will cover the following topics on blockchain:

- A genealogical analogy for blockchain
- The Bitcoin consensus mechanism
- A brief discussion of Hyperledger
- Blockchain evolution

The genealogy analogy

One of the authors recently attended a Chinese university alma mater reunion event in Beijing, where blockchain became a hot discussion topic. A very well-regarded schoolmate and scholar, Professor Yang, who has authored books on cryptography and public data safeguards, used genealogy to describe a blockchain. This is a well-thought-out analogy since it explains blockchain intuitively and easily. The analogy is borrowed here to illustrate the basic ideas behind the technology.

Back in the old days in China, it was a custom for each family of a clan (sharing the same last name) to keep a copy of the genealogical tree of the clan. When members of a family changed due to either marriage or the birth of an offspring, as well as adoption, the new member's name would appear in each copy. However, the new member had to be accepted by the clan before the name could be added in. There were cases when a marriage was not endorsed by a majority of the clan due to various reasons. In this case, the new member's name would not be entered into the genealogy. In other words, when a new member joined in a family, the news was broadcast to other families of the clan. If the clan reached a consensus on accepting the new member, each family would update their copy of the genealogical tree to reflect the change. On the other hand, if the clan decided not to accept the new member, the name would not be added in. The genealogy could be used for verification purposes. For example, if a stranger made a claim to be a member of the clan, or two people with the same last name were eager to find out whether they shared the same ancestor, with the genealogy, it was easy to verify this. The outcome would be accepted since the genealogy was considered reliable thanks to the aforementioned consensus and decentralized records, which were difficult to manipulate unless the majority of families agreed.

A blockchain shares many of the characteristics of a genealogy. They are summarized as follows:

- Like a clan consisting of many related families, a blockchain network consists of nodes. Each node is like a family.
- Like every family keeping a copy of the clan's genealogy, each node of a blockchain maintains a copy of all transactions that have occurred on the chain, starting from the very beginning. The collection of all transactions is a **ledger**. This makes a blockchain a decentralized data repository.

- A genealogy starts with a common ancestor of the clan and names with direct relationships, such as parents and children, that are connected by a line for linkage. Similarly, a ledger consists of blocks. Each block contains one or multiple transactions depending on the type of blockchain. (As you will see later, blocks on Bitcoin or Ethereum host multiple transactions, while R3's Corda uses a block with only one transaction). Transactions are like names, and a block is similar to the invisible box containing a couple's names. An equivalent of the root ancestor is called the **genesis block**, which is the first block of a blockchain. Similar to a line linking parents and children, a hash, which will later be explained in more detail, points from the current block to its ancestor block.
- Like the consensus mechanism for adding new names to a genealogy, the Bitcoin blockchain uses a mechanism called Proof-of-Work to decide whether a block can be added to the chain. Like a genealogy, after a block is added to a chain, it is difficult to change (hack) unless one possesses the majority (which is called a 51% attack) of the computing power of the network.
- Genealogy provides transparency in a clan's history. Similarly, a blockchain allows a user to query the whole ledger or just a part of the ledger and find out about coin movements.
- Since every family kept a copy of the genealogy, it was unlikely to lose the genealogy even if many copies were lost due to a natural disaster, a war, or other reasons. As long as at least one family survived, the genealogy survived. Similarly, a decentralized ledger will survive as long as at least one node survives.

While genealogy is a good analogy to explain some key concepts of a blockchain, they are not the same. Inevitably, there are features that are not shared by them. For example, the blockchain uses cryptography and hashes extensively for data protection and deterring hackers. A genealogy does not have such a need. Therefore, next we move away from the genealogy analogy and explain key blockchain concepts chronically.

Bitcoin

Blockchain technology initially caught people's attention due to the **Bitcoin** blockchain, an idea outlined by a white paper authored by Satoshi Nakamoto and published in October 2008 on the cryptography mailing list at metzdowd.com. It describes the **Bitcoin digital currency** (**BTC**) and was titled *Bitcoin: A Peer-to-Peer Electronic Cash System*. In January 2009, Satoshi Nakamoto released the first Bitcoin software, which launched the network and the first units of the Bitcoin cryptocurrency: BTC coins.

Why Bitcoin

The creation of Bitcoin was right after the 2008 financial crisis, the most severe economic crisis since the Great Depression. This is not coincidental. The inventor of the Bitcoin cryptocurrency aimed at addressing people's disillusionment with financial institutions, whose epic failures in risk controls resulted in the 2008 financial crisis.

A fundamental role played by financial institutions is to be an intermediary entity and bring untrusting parties together to facilitate transactions. For example, a retail bank attracts residual money from individuals and lends to individuals or companies that need the money. The difference in interest paid to the money suppliers and borrowers is the fee a bank charges for providing the intermediary service. Financial institutions are very successful in providing these services and play a pivotal role in powering economies worldwide. However, there are many deficiencies associated with this business model. Here are some examples:

- **Slow**: It often takes days to complete a financial transaction. For instance, it takes three days (after an order is initially entered) to complete and settle a cross-border money transfer. To make it happen, multiple departments and application systems within an institution and across institutions have to work together to facilitate the transaction. Another example is stock trading. An investor hires a broker to enter an order to be routed to a stock exchange. Here, the broker is either a member of the exchange or routes the order to another intermediary institution with membership. After a match is found between a buyer and a seller at the exchange, the transaction details are recorded by two parties who send it to their back offices respectively. The back-office teams work with a clearing house for clearance and settlement. It takes T + 3 for both parties to complete the action of exchanging ownership of the security (stock) and the cash.
- **Expensive**: Financial intermediaries often charge hefty fees when providing these services. For example, a US bank could charge $10 to $30 USD to serve an individual by sending money from the US to a receiver in another country. In the case of stock trading, a full-service broker often charges tens of USD or more for a transaction. Even with a discount broker, an investor needs to pay $7 to $10 USD per transaction.
- **Prone to be hacked**: Since details on a customer and the transactions are saved in a centralized area within an institution, it is prone to being hacked and causing severe financial loss or leakage of confidential personal information about customers. Recently, there have been high-profile personal data leakage incidents at reputable companies such as JP Morgan (83 million accounts hacked in 2014), Target (up to 70 million customers' information hacked in 2013), and Equifax (148 million US consumers' information hacked in 2017).

- **Not transparent**: Financial institutions keep both detailed and aggregated information on transactions. However, most of the information is not open to the individual customer and this results in information imparity. In the example of cross-border money transfers, both the sender and receiver have to wait for three days to know whether the transaction has been completed successfully or not. If a transaction fails, a lengthy investigation has to be triggered. Imagine if the receiver was in an emergency and needed the funding immediately. Such a service is unsatisfactory despite the client having to pay a high fee.

With blockchain technology, the preceding problems are resolved elegantly. In the case of the Bitcoin blockchain, the underlying asset to be transferred is the digital coin, BTC. A cross-border BTC transaction can complete in no more than 1 hour. No settlement is needed since transaction and settlement are in one action. The cost of this transaction is a tiny fraction of a transfer via a bank. For example, a recent report published by the **Bank of America** (**BoA**) claims a transfer via blockchain costs 1/6000 of what BoA charges. However, for some clients, waiting an hour is still too long. **Ripple**, a payment provider for sending money globally, completes in under 1 minute.

The word Bitcoin often causes confusion as people use the word interchangeably for three things: the cryptocurrency, the blockchain, and the protocol. To avoid this confusion, we use BTC to refer to the cryptocurrency, and Bitcoin to refer to the blockchain and the corresponding network that uses the distributed ledger. For the protocol, we will fully spell out **Bitcoin protocol** or simply protocol.

A peer-to-peer network

To explain how Bitcoin works, let's look at what steps are involved with the existing business model for completing a cross-border transaction:

- A customer enters an order either by visiting a bank branch or via the web. The sender provides detailed information of an order such as the amount, sending currency, receiver name, receiving currency, receiver's bank name, account and branch numbers, and a SWIFT number. Here, **SWIFT** stands for the **Society for Worldwide Interbank Financial Telecommunications**, a messaging network used by financial institutions to transmit information and instructions securely through a standardized system of codes. SWIFT assigns each financial organization a unique code called, interchangeably, the **bank identifier code** (**BIC**), SWIFT code, SWIFT ID, or ISO 9362 code.
- The sending bank takes the order and verifies that the sender has sufficient funds available.

- The bank charges a fee and converts the remaining amount from the sending currency to an amount in the receiving currency by executing an FX transaction.
- The sending bank enters a transferring message to SWIFT with all the needed information.
- Upon receiving the message, the receiving bank verifies the receiver's account information.
- Upon a successful verification and settling the funds between sending and receiving banks following the protocol, the receiving bank credits the amount to the receiver's account.

Since there are multiple steps, entities, and systems involved, the preceding activities take days to complete.

A Bitcoin network connects computers around the world. Each computer is a **node** with equal status, except for a subset of nodes called **miners**, which choose to play the role of verifying transactions, building blocks and linking to the chain. With Bitcoin, the business model for completing a money transfer involves the following steps:

1. A sender enters the number of BTCs, the addresses of Bitcoins to be taken from, and addresses of Bitcoins to be transferred to, using an **e-wallet.**
2. The transaction request is sent to the Bitcoin network by the e-wallet.
3. After miners have successfully verified the transaction and committed it to the network, the BTCs are now available for use by the receiver.

The Bitcoin transfer is a lot faster (in 1 hour, or minutes if using Ripple) for the following reasons:

- The transaction and settlement are one step. This avoids the need to go through a time-consuming and expensive reconciliation process.
- No FX trade is needed since BTC is borderless. It can move worldwide freely and rapidly.
- No fund settlement is needed between banks since the transaction requires no intermediary banks.

In a case where a sender or receiver prefers to use a **fiat currency** such as USD, GBP, CNY, or JPY, a cryptocurrency market can be used for a conversion between BTC and a fiat currency. A website, CoinMarketCap, lists these markets: `https://coinmarketcap.com/rankings/exchanges/`. As of September 21, 2018, there are 14,044 markets. In terms of market capitalization, the top three are Binance (`https://www.binance.com/`), OKEx (`https://www.binance.com/`), and Huopi (`https://www.huobi.pro`).

A peer-to-peer network can connect nodes worldwide. However, a merely physical connection is not enough to make two untrusting parties trade with each other. To allow them to trade, Bitcoin takes the following measures:

- Every node saves a complete copy of all transactions in a decentralized ledger. This makes any alteration to a transaction on the chain infeasible.
- The ledger transactions are grouped in blocks. A non-genesis block is linked to its previous block by saving the hash of all preceding blocks' transactions. Consequently, changing a transaction requires changing the current block of transactions and all subsequent blocks. This makes hacking the decentralized ledger extremely difficult.
- Bitcoin addresses the double-spending issue, that is the same BTC being spent twice, by using the Proof-of-Work consensus algorithm.
- Hashes are used extensively to protect the identities of parties and detect any changes occurring in a block.
- Public/private keys and addresses are used to mask the identities of trading parties and to sign a transaction digitally .

With these measures, untrusting parties feel comfortable to trade due to these reasons:

- The transaction is immutable and permanent. Neither party can nullify a transaction unilaterally.
- No double spending is possible.
- Transaction and settlement occur simultaneously; therefore, there is no settlement risk.
- Identities are protected.
- Transactions are signed by both parties, which will avoid any future legal disputes.

Cryptography and hash functions

Cryptography or cryptology is research on techniques for securing communication in the presence of adversaries. In the old days, cryptography was synonymous with encryption. Modern cryptography relies heavily on mathematical theory and computer science. It also utilizes works from other disciplines such as electrical engineering, communications science, and physics.

Cryptographic algorithms are designed around the assumption that with foreseeable computational hardware advances, it will not be feasible for any adversary to decipher encrypted messages based on these algorithms. In other words, in theory, it is possible to decode the encrypted message, but it is infeasible to do so practically. These algorithms are therefore defined to be computationally secure. Theoretical research (for instance, parallel or integer factorization algorithms) and computational technology advancements (for instance, quantum computers) can make these algorithms practically insecure and, therefore, encryption algorithms need to be adapted continuously.

Encryption is the process of converting plaintext into unintelligible text, called ciphertext. Decryption is the reverse, in other words moving from the unintelligible ciphertext back to plaintext.

The encryption algorithms used by Bitcoin mining are hash functions. A hash function is a function that maps data of any size to data of a fixed size. The values returned by a hash function are called hash values or simply hashes. A cryptographic hash function allows one to verify easily that some input data maps to a given hash value. However, the reverse – when the input data is unknown—it is practically infeasible to reconstruct the input plaintext from a hash value. In other words, hashing is a one-way operation. Another notable attribute of a hashing function is that a minor change in the input plaintext will result in a completely different hash value. This feature is desirable for safeguarding information as any tiny change to the original data by a hacker results in a visibly different hash.

Two common hash algorithms are MD5 (message-digest algorithm 5) and SHA-1 (secure hash algorithm):

- Developed by Ronald Rivest in 1991, MD5 maps input plaintext into a 128-bit resulting hash value. MD5 Message-Digest checksums are commonly used to validate data integrity when digital files are transferred or stored. MD5 has been found to suffer from extensive vulnerabilities.

- SHA-1 is a cryptographic hash function mapping input plaintext into a 160-bit (20-byte) hash known as a message digest – often displayed as a hexadecimal number, 40 digits long. SHA-1 was designed by the United States national security agency and is a US federal information processing standard.

SHA-256 is a successor hash function to SHA-1. It is one of the strongest hash functions available and has not yet been compromised in any way. SHA-256 generates an almost unique 256-bit (32-byte) signature for a text. For example, *My test string* maps to `5358c37942b0126084bb16f7d602788d00416e01bc3fd0132f4458d d355d8e76`. With a small change, the hash of *My test strings* is `98ff9f0555435 f792339d6b7bf5fbcca82f1a83fde2bb76f6aa95d66050887cc`, a completely different value. SHA-256 produces 2^256 possible hashes. There is yet to be a case where two different inputs have produced the same SHA-256 hash, an issue called collision in cryptography. Even with the fastest supercomputer, it will take longer than the age of our universe to hit a collision. As a result, SHA-256 is used by Bitcoin for encryption.

The distributed ledger, blocks, transactions, addresses, and UTXO

At a financial institution, a ledger is a book for recording financial transactions. Similarly, Bitcoin maintains a ledger for bookkeeping BTC transactions and balances by address. One key difference is that a bank's ledger is centralized and Bitcoin's ledger is decentralized. Consequently, a bank's ledger is much easier to be cooked. On the other side, Bitcoin's ledger is very difficult to cook as one has to change the ledger at all nodes worldwide.

A user submits a transaction containing the following information:

- Sources of the BTCs to be transferred from
- The amount of BTCs to be transferred
- Destinations the BTCs should be transferred to

As per the Wiki site, a transaction has a general structure shown as follows:

General format of a Bitcoin transaction (inside a block)

Field	Description	Size
Version no	currently 1	4 bytes
Flag	If present, always 0001, and indicates the presence of witness data	optional 2 byte array
In-counter	positive integer VI = VarInt	1 - 9 bytes
list of inputs	the first input of the first transaction is also called "coinbase" (its content was ignored in earlier versions)	<in-counter>-many inputs
Out-counter	positive integer VI = VarInt	1 - 9 bytes
list of outputs	the outputs of the first transaction spend the mined bitcoins for the block	<out-counter>-many outputs
Witnesses	A list of witnesses, 1 for each input, omitted if flag above is missing	variable, see Segregated_Witness
lock_time	if non-zero and sequence numbers are < 0xFFFFFFFF: block height or timestamp when transaction is final	4 bytes

Both source and destination addresses are 64-character hashes. Here is an example of an address: `979e6b063b436438105895939f4ff13d068428d2f71312cf5594c132905bfxy1`.

The term *address* is a bit confusing. A programmer may think it to be an address related to a disk or memory location. However, it has nothing to do with a physical location. Instead, it is a logical label for grouping BTCs that have been transferred from/to it. In a way, one can think of it as a bank account number, yet there are fundamental differences between them. For example, a bank has a centralized place where metadata on an account, for instance, owner name, account open date, and account type, is saved. In addition, the account balance is precalculated and saved. In Bitcoin, there is no metadata on an address and one has to query the entire ledger to find the balance of an address by counting the net BTCs being transferred in and out of the address. Addresses are referred to only in Bitcoin transactions. When the balance of an address falls to 0, any future request for taking BTCs from the address will fail the transaction validation due to insufficient funds.

Bitcoin utilizes the **UTXO** model to manage its BTC transfer. The term was introduced by cryptocurrency, where it refers to an *unspent transaction output*. This is an output of a blockchain transaction that has not been spent and can be used as an input for a future transaction. In a Bitcoin transaction, only unspent outputs can be used as an input, which helps to prevent double spending and fraud. As a result, a committed transaction results in deleting inputs on a blockchain and creating outputs in the form of UTXOs. The newly created unspent transaction outputs can be spent by the owner holding the corresponding private keys. In other words, UTXOs are processed continuously and a committed transaction leads to removing spent coins and creating new unspent coins in the UTXO database.

Like an address, a BTC is not associated with any physical object such as a digital token file or a physically minted coin. Instead, it only exists in transactions in the distributed ledger. For example, if one wants to know the total number of BTCs minted so far, one has to go through all nonzero balance addresses on the blockchain and add up all the BTCs. Since every node of Bitcoin keeps a copy of the ledger, it is only a matter of taking computing time to find an answer.

When a user enters a BTC transaction request at a node, Bitcoin software installed at the node broadcasts the transaction to all nodes. Nodes on the network will verify the validity of the transaction by retrieving all historical transactions containing the input addresses and ensuring that BTCs from these addresses are legitimate and sufficient. After that, the mining nodes start to construct a block by collecting the verified transactions. Normally, a Bitcoin block contains between 1,500 to 2,000 transactions. A miner who wins the race to resolve a difficult mathematical puzzle gets the role to build and link a new block to the chain. On the Bitcoin blockchain, a new block is created around every 10 minutes. As of September 21, 2018, approximately 542,290 blocks have been created on Bitcoin. The structure of a Bitcoin block is shown as follows:

Block structure

Field	Description	Size
Magic no	value always 0xD9B4BEF9	4 bytes
Blocksize	number of bytes following up to end of block	4 bytes
Blockheader	consists of 6 items	80 bytes
Transaction counter	positive integer VI = VarInt	1 - 9 bytes
transactions	the (non empty) list of transactions	<Transaction counter>-many transactions

Here, the block header contains the following fields:

Field	Purpose	Updated when...	Size (Bytes)
Version	Block version number	You upgrade the software and it specifies a new version	4
hashPrevBlock	256-bit hash of the previous block header	A new block comes in	32
hashMerkleRoot	256-bit hash based on all of the transactions in the block	A transaction is accepted	32
Time	Current timestamp as seconds since 1970-01-01T00:00 UTC	Every few seconds	4
Bits	Current target in compact format	The difficulty is adjusted	4
Nonce	32-bit number (starts at 0)	A hash is tried (increments)	4

The concept of a **nonce** will be explained in the subsection on mining. **hashPrevBlock** is the same value as **hashMerkleRoot**. The Merkle tree hash root is essentially the hash of all transaction hashes in the block via a binary tree aggregation structure. The following diagram explains the idea:

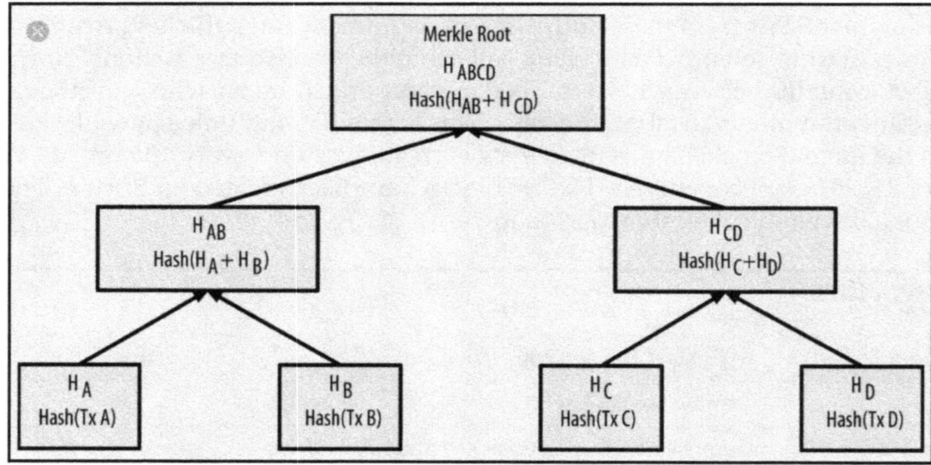

The consensus mechanism

If someone buys a bottle of water for $1, that person cannot spend the same $1 to buy a can of coke. If a person is free to double-spend a dollar, money would be worthless since everyone would have unlimited amounts and the scarcity, which gives the currency its value, would disappear. This is called the **double-spending problem**. With BTC, double spending is the act of using the same Bitcoin more than once. If this problem is not resolved, BTC loses its scarcity and cannot be used to facilitate a trade between two untrusting parties. The Bitcoin Core network protects against double spends via a consensus mechanism. To explain how the Bitcoin consensus mechanism works, we first describe the concepts of **PoW** (**Proof-of-Work**) and mining.

As explained earlier, a miner needs to solve a difficult mathematical puzzle ahead of other miners in order to receive the role of being a builder of the current new block and receive a reward for doing the work. The work of resolving the math problem is called **PoW**.

Why is PoW needed? Think of this: in a network consisting of mutually untrusting parties, more honest parties are needed than dishonest attackers in order to make the network function. Imagine if upon collecting sufficient transactions for a new block, a miner is allowed to build the new block immediately. This simply becomes a race for whoever can put enough transactions together quickly. This leaves a door wide open for malicious attackers to hack the network by including invalid or fake transactions and always win the race. This would allow hackers to double-spend BTCs freely.

Therefore, to prevent attackers from introducing bad transactions, a sufficient window of time is needed for participating nodes to verify every transaction's validity by making sure a BTC has not been spent yet. Since every node maintains a copy of the ledger, an honest miner can trace the history and ensure the following to confirm the validity of a transaction:

- The requestor of a transaction does own the BTCs.
- The same BTCs have not been spent by any other transactions in the ledger.
- The same BTCs have not been spent by other transactions within the candidate block.

This window of time is currently set to be around 10 minutes. To enforce the 10-minute waiting time, Bitcoin asks a miner to solve a sufficiently difficult mathematical puzzle. The puzzle requires only a simple computation. Miners have to repeat the same computation many times in order to burn enough CPU time to reach the network's goal of building a new block every 10 minutes on average. The process of repeated guessing is called **mining** and the device (specially made) is called a **mining rig**.

Since, in order to win the mining race, a miner needs to invest heavily in hardware, these miners are dedicated to the work of mining and aim to receive sufficient BTCs to cover the cost of running the mining operation and make a profit. As of the first half of 2018, the reward given to a winning miner is 12.5 BTCs. One can find the price of BTC by visiting the CoinMarketCap website (`https://coinmarketcap.com/`). As of September 21, 2018, one BTC is traded at around $6,710. Therefore, 12.5 BTC is worth about $83,875 USD.

Per Bitcoin protocol, mining is the only way for a new BTC to be issued (minted). Having a miner be rewarded handsomely serves three purposes:

- Compensates a miner's investment on hardware.
- Covers mining operational costs such as utility bills, which can be significant due to the large mining rigs being deployed at a mining site, human salaries, and site rentals.
- Gives miners incentives to safeguard the network from being attacked by malicious hackers. Miners are motivated to maintain the Bitcoin network in order not to lose value in their BTCs and their mining infrastructure. If Bitcoin is breached by hackers, Bitcoin's reputation will suffer badly and BTC prices would freefall. This is exactly what the Bitcoin inventor hoped for: having more good miners than bad miners to address the double-spending issue.

The total number of BTC that can be issued is fixed to be 21 million. As of today (September 19, 2018), around 17 million BTCs have been issued. The Bitcoin protocol defines a rule for dynamically adjusting the payout rate and the remaining 4 million coins aren't expected to be mined completely for another 122 years. The following point explains how the block creation payout rate is dynamically adjusted:

- The rate changes at every 210,000 blocks. It is a function of block height on the chain with genesis=0, and is calculated using 64-bit integer operations such as: (50 * 100000000) >> (height / 210000). The rate initially started with 50 BTCs, and fell to 25 BTCs at block 210,000. It fell to 12.5 BTCs at block 420,000, and will eventually go down to 0 when the network reaches 6,930,000 blocks.

Forking

A Bitcoin blockchain can diverge into two potential paths since miners do not necessarily collect transactions and contract block candidates in the same way, nor at the same time. Other reasons such as hacking or software upgrades can also lead to path divergence. The splitting patches are called **forks**. There are temporary forks and permanent forks.

If a permanent fork occurs due to, for example, malicious attacks, a hard fork occurs. Similarly, there is the concept of soft fork. Both hard fork and soft fork refer to a radical change to the protocol. Hard fork makes previously invalid blocks/transactions valid and a soft fork makes previously valid blocks/transactions invalid.

To remove a temporary fork, Bitcoin protocol dictates that the longest chain should be used. In other words, when facing two paths, a winning miner will choose the longer chain to link a new block. As a result, the longer path continues to grow and the blocks on the losing (shorter) path becomes orphaned. Bitcoin nodes will soon discard or not take the orphaned blocks. They only keep the blocks on the longest chain as being the valid blocks.

In the case of a permanent fork, nodes on the network have to choose which chain to follow. For example, Bitcoin Cash diverged from Bitcoin due to a disagreement within the Bitcoin community on how to handle the scalability problem. As a result, Bitcoin Cash became its own chain and shares the transaction history from the genesis block up to the forking point. As of September 21, Bitcoin Cash's market cap is around $8 billion, ranking fourth, versus Bitcoin's $215 billion.

Mining and difficulty level

There is one more issue that needs to be resolved: how to maintain the new block building rate of 10 minutes. If nothing is done, the mining rate will change due to the following factors:

- The number of miners on the network can vary in response to the BTC price
- Technology advancements make mining rigs progressively faster
- The total number of mining rigs varies

Bitcoin adjusts the **difficulty level** of the mathematical puzzle in order to keep the building rate at 10 minutes. The difficulty level is calculated from the rate at which the most recent blocks were added in. If the average rate of new blocks being added is less than 10 minutes, the difficulty level will be increased. If the average rate takes more than 10 minutes, it's decreased. The difficulty level is updated every 2,016 blocks. The following graph displays the historical trend in Bitcoin difficulty level.

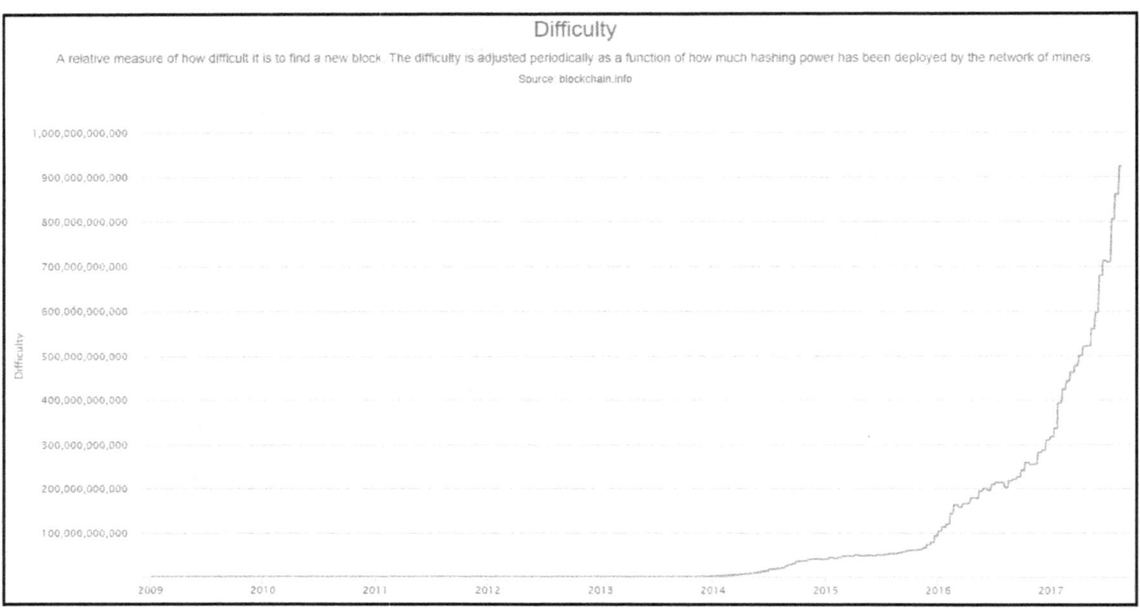

We have yet to talk about the actual mining algorithm. Assume the current difficulty level is to find the first hash value with the leading character to be 0. In Bitcoin, the process of solving a puzzle, that is, mining, requires a miner to follow these steps:

- First, find the SHA-256 hash of the block in construction.
- If the resulting hash has a leading 0, the miner solves the puzzle. The miner links the block to the ledger on the node and claims the trophy, 12.5 BTCs. The miner's node broadcasts the news to all nodes. All other nodes and miners on the network validate the answer (by mapping the block information plus nonce to get the same hash) and validate the entire history of the ledger, making sure that the block contains valid transactions.
- If it passes the checks, all nodes on the network add the block to their copies of the ledger. Miners start to work on the next new block.

- If the winning miner is a malicious attacker and includes bad transactions in the block, the validation of these transactions will fail and other miners will not include the block in their ledger copies. They will continue to mine on the current block. As time passes, the path containing the bad block will no longer be the longest path and, therefore, the bad block will become an orphaned block. This is essentially how all nodes on the network reach consensus to add only good blocks to the network and prevent bad blocks from sneaking in, therefore resolving the double-spending issue.
- If the resulting hash does not start with 0, then the miner is allowed to append a sequence number, known to be a nonce, starting from 0 to the input text, and retry the hash.
- If the resulting hash still does not contain a leading 0, the miner will add another sequence number, 1, to the input text and obtain a new hash. The miner will keep trying in this way until it finds the first hash with a leading zero.

The following is an example of how the plaintext and nonce work together. The original plaintext is *input string* and the nonce varies from 0 to 1:

- **input string**: `f23f4781d6814ebe349c6b230c1f700714f4f70f735022bd4b1fb69421859993`
- **input string0**: `5db70bb3ae36e5b87415c1c9399100bc60f2068a2b0ec04536e92ad2598b6bbb`
- **input string1**: `5d0a0f2c69b88343ba44d64168b350ef62ce4e0da73044557bff451fd5df6e96`

In Bitcoin, *adjusting difficult level* largely refers to changing the required number of leading zeros. (The actual adjustment involves some other miner tuning to the requirement.) Each addition of a leading zero will increase the average number of tries significantly and therefore will increase the computing time. This is how Bitcoin manages to maintain the average rate of 10 minutes for new blocks being added in. The current Bitcoin difficulty level is 18 leading zeros.

Hacking – the 51% problem

Thanks to the rising price of BTC, the mining operation has become more attractive. Investments are rushing in and large mining pools involving thousands of rigs or more have joined the network in order to gain an advantage in the race to solve the puzzle first and get the reward. For players without large capital from investments, they have a choice to participate in a mining pool. When the pool wins a race, the award will be allocated to each participant based on the computational power contributed.

This ever-growing computational power of a pool poses a real threat due to the so-called **51% problem**. This problem occurs when a miner manages to build up computational power to total at least 51% of the total computing power of the network. When this occurs, the miner will have a chance to outrun other miners. The miner can continue to grow the ledger with blocks containing bad transactions since this miner has more than a 50% chance of solving the puzzle first. Soon, the malicious miner's ledger will grow to be the longest path and all other nodes have to save this path based on Bitcoin's consensus protocol.

For a large and well-established network such as Bitcoin, the 51% problem is not as critical an issue, mainly due to the following reasons:

- A well-established network will attract a much larger number of participating parties and connect a very significant number of nodes. It will take an exorbitantly high initial investment for a hacker to purchase the necessary mining rigs. When such a network is attacked, the price of cryptography will drop quickly when the news becomes public and the hacker will have a low chance of recovering the investment.
- In the history of Bitcoin, there have been cases when a mining pool that accumulated dangerously high computing power approached this line. When the participating miners in the pool realized the problem, many of them chose to leave the pool. Soon, the computational power of the pool fell to a safe level.
- In the case of a small and immature network, it is not difficult for a miner to muster computing power of more than 51%. However, the cryptocurrency value of these networks is minimal and it gives hackers very little financial incentive to take advantage of the 51% problem.

Private keys and Bitcoin wallets

As discussed earlier, BTCs do not physically exist. The only evidence of their existence is when they are associated with addresses, which are referred to in transactions. When an address is initially created, a pair of public and private keys are generated with it. The public key is made known to the public and the private key is kept only by the owner of the address. When the owner wants to spend all or a portion of their BTCs, the owner provides a digital signature signed with the private key and sends the BTC request to the Bitcoin network. In other words, one has to know both the address and its private key to spend the BTC.

If an owner loses a private key, its associated BTCs will be lost permanently. Therefore, it is advised to keep this information in a safe place. It is generally good practice to keep the address and private keys in separate places. To prevent a digital copy getting lost, an owner should maintain physical copies of printouts. To make conversion easier, an owner can print a QR code and later scan the QR code whenever it is needed.

Bitcoin wallet applications are available to help a user manage keys and addresses. One can use a wallet to do the following:

- Generate addresses and corresponding public/private keys
- Save and organize a BTC's information
- Send a transaction request to the Bitcoin network

In Bitcoin, a private key is a 256-bit-long hash and a public key is 512 bits long. They can be converted into shorter lengths in hexadecimal representation. The following screenshot gives an example of a pair of public/private keys along with an address:

```
Private key:
a7f9c7ad318014b11cbad0a18587b374c339d91f55ca64c4c5e067776d0b65cb

Public key:
04d8fc7523fcd7caa825b6ed97d8564c78f59e8ba903bff5fe1e3c096a45d435937
942616f4dbccb353d3e19e822d707996143a603a6273cf237acfaf5bd029874

Wif:  5K6GJ5y9qSDSmrGZ1idLbWoXk4iaJpxFuDpiCC78cgngCXTSeDv

Address:  1GnUipq7cTjiPxEsCDzW6nYgbUyRa7eFYm
```

Bitcoin private keys can also be expressed in a string of 51 characters starting with a 5 and a public key in a string of 72 characters. A sample private key is `5Jd54v5mVLvyRsjDGTFbTZFGvwLosYKayRosbLYMxZFBLfEpXnp` and a sample public key is `BFCDB2DCE28D959F2815B16F81798483ADA7726A3C4655DA4FBFC0E1108A8FD17B448A68`.

Bitcoin scripting

One can install the following development tools for programming Bitcoin operations:

- **NodeJS**: This is an open source, cross-platform JavaScript runtime environment that executes JavaScript code outside of a browser. It allows a programmer to write and execute scripts quickly and easily. These scripts can be written to be run in a web browser or on a server.
- **BitcoinJS**: This is a JavaScript library for working with Bitcoin and its cryptographic functions. BitcoinJS can be used to generate public/private keys and addresses.
- **Blockchain.info**: This is a public API that can be used to query the blockchain to find out balances and broadcast transactions to the network. It can be used to implement a Bitcoin node and install and run a Bitcoin node.

After installing the preceding tools, one can execute the following operations:

- Generate a new private key and compute a public key
- Check the balance for a certain address
- Generate addresses
- Construct a new transaction
- Send a transaction, which involves three steps:
    - Build a transaction with a list of inputs and outputs
    - Sign the transaction with the required private keys
    - Broadcast the transaction to the network
- Build an escrow account
- Broadcasts the transaction

Altcoins

Thanks to Bitcoin, blockchain technology has attracted worldwide attention. Like any new technology, it has its limitations. Many variations of Bitcoin were created to address a particular limitation of Bitcoin. Here, we mention a few of them:

- **Bitcoin Cash**: This is a hard fork of the Bitcoin chain that was created because a group of Bitcoin core developers wanted to use a different way of addressing the scalability issue.
- **Litecoin**: This is almost identical to Bitcoin except that the time for adding a new block was reduced from 10 minutes to 2 minutes.
- **Zcash**: This is based on Bitcoin but offers total payment confidentiality.
- **Monero and Zcash**: Both altcoins address the privacy issue by making transaction history untraceable, but they implement two different solutions.
- **Dash**: This mainly improves user-friendliness. For example, transactions are made untraceable and a user does not have to wait for several additional new blocks to be added before considering a transaction to be committed to the chain.
- **Namecoin**: This extends the use case of Bitcoin, which is for trading BTCs only, to providing domain name services.
- **Peercoin**: This altcoin addresses the deficiencies of PoW, which is environmentally unfriendly and is low in throughput. Instead, it adopts proof of stake for achieving consensus. Based on this rule, a miner validates block transactions according to how many coins a miner holds. In other words, the mining power of a miner is in proportion to the number of peercoins owned.
- **Primecoin**: A primecoin miner competes to be the first to find the next biggest prime number.

Ethereum

Regardless of the efforts made from the steps-mentioned altcoins in addressing some part of the Bitcoin's limitations, there are several fundamental issues that are not being addressed yet:

- Bitcoin and these altcoins are specific to one purpose: trading either BTC or an altcoin.
- Although a programmer can use tools such as BitcoinJS to interact with the network, the resulting code sits outside of the blockchain and is not guaranteed to run. The chain itself does not have a Turing complete programming language for coding directly on a blockchain.

- These blockchains are stateless and one has to search through the entire ledger to find an answer such as the total number of BTC minted.

In response to these problems, Vitalik Buterin, a Canadian cryptocurrency researcher and programmer, proposed the idea of Ethereum in late 2013. Funded by an online crowdsale, the system went live on 30 July 2015, with 11.9 million coins *premined* for the crowdsale.

The core idea for Ethereum was to build a general-purpose blockchain so users could solve a wide range of business problems not just limited to cryptocurrency transfer. Ethereum introduced a few new and critical concepts:

- The concept of saving a smart contract on a blockchain
- The concept of implementing a smart contract with a Turing complete programming language such as Solidity and running the piece of code on the blockchain

Solidity was initially proposed in August 2014 by Gavin Wood. The Ethereum project's Solidity team led by Christian Reitwiessner later developed the language. It is one of the five languages, (Solidity, Serpent, LLL, Vyper, and Mutan) designed to target the **Ethereum virtual machine** (**EVM**).

Nick Szabo, a programmer and lawyer, initially proposed the term *smart contract* in 1996. In his blog, Nick Szabo described it as the granddaddy of all smart contracts, the vending machine.
A vending machine shares the exact same properties as a smart contract on a blockchain today. A vending machine is built with hardcoded rules that define what actions to execute when certain conditions are fulfilled, for example:

- If Susan inputs a dollar bill in the vending machine, then she will receive a bag of pretzels.
- If Tom puts in a five-dollar bill, Tom will receive a bag of pretzels and also change of four dollars.

In other words, rules are defined and enforced by a vending machine physically. Similarly, a smart contract contains rules in program code that are run on the blockchain and triggered when certain conditions are met.

The introduction of the smart contract concept is significant:

- A smart contract is a scripted legal document.
- The code built into the contract is stored on the Ethereum blockchain and cannot be tampered with or removed. This greatly increases the credibility of the legal document.

- This code cannot be stopped, meaning any party—regardless of how powerful the party is—cannot order or interfere with the running of the smart contract code. As long as certain conditions are met, the code will run and the legally defined actions will be fulfilled.
- Ethereum to blockchain is like an OS to a computer. In other words, the platform is generic, no longer serving only one specific purpose.
- It now has a Turing complete language: Solidity.

Enterprise blockchain – Hyperledger

The arrival of Ethereum revolutionized blockchain technology. Applying technology to resolve business problems well beyond the financial industry has become feasible. However, there are many scenarios where Ethereum is not enough. Ethereum's issues include the following:

- Real enterprise applications, particularly in the financial industry, require a high throughput, which can mean billions of transactions a day. The current form of Ethereum has a maximum capacity of 1.4 million a day. Bitcoin is even worse: 300,000 transactions a day. During a stress test, Bitcoin Cash reached 2.2 million. Ethereum 2.0 under development aims at getting to a billion transactions a day while maintaining a decentralized and secure public blockchain.
- Many financial markets, for instance OTC Derivatives or FX, are permission-based. A public blockchain supported by Ethereum or Bitcoin does not meet such a need.

To satisfy their needs, well-established companies across industries form consortiums to work on enterprise blockchain projects, which are permission-based only. In other words, a node has to receive approval before it can join in the blockchain network. Examples of enterprise blockchains are Hyperledger and R3's Corda.

In December 2015, the **Linux Foundation** (**LF**) announced the creation of the Hyperledger Project. Its objective is to advance cross-industry collaboration by developing blockchains and distributed ledgers. On 12 July 2017, the project announced its production-ready **Hyperledger Fabric** (**HF**) 1.0.

Currently, Hyperledger includes five blockchain frameworks:

- **Hyperledger Fabric** (**HF**): A permissioned blockchain, initially contributed by IBM and Digital Asset, it is designed to be a foundation for developing applications or solutions with a modular architecture. It takes plugin components for providing functionalities such as consensus and membership services. Like Ethereum, HF can host and execute smart contracts, which are named chaincode. An HF network consists of peer nodes, which execute smart contracts (chaincode), query ledger data, validate transactions, and interact with applications. User-entered transactions are channeled to an ordering service component, which initially serves to be HF's consensus mechanism. Special nodes called Orderer nodes validate the transactions, ensure the consistency of the blockchain, and send the validated transactions to the peers of the network as well as to **membership service provider** (**MSP**) services that are implemented to be a certificate authority.
- **Hyperledger Iroha**: Based on HF, it is designed for mobile applications. Iroha was contributed by Soramitsu, Hitachi, NTT Data, and Colu. It features a modern and domain-driven C++ design. It implements a consensus algorithm called Sumeragi.
- **Hyperledger Burrow**: Contributed initially by Monax and Intel, Burrow is a modular blockchain that was client-built to follow EVM specifications.
- **Hyperledger Sawtooth**: Contributed by Intel, it implemented a consensus algorithm called **Proof of Elapsed Time** (**PoET**). PoET is designed to achieve distributed consensus as efficiently as possible. Sawtooth supports both permissioned and permissionless networks. Sawtooth is designed for versatility.
- **Hyperledger Indy**: Contributed initially by the Sovrin foundation, it is intended to support independent identity on distributed ledgers. Indy provides tools, libraries, and reusable components, which are implemented to provide digital identities.

Early members of the initiative include the following:

- Blockchain ISVs, (Blockchain, ConsenSys, Digital Asset, R3, Onchain)
- Technology platform companies such as Cisco, Fujitsu, Hitachi, IBM, Intel, NEC, NTT DATA, Red Hat, and VMware
- Financial institutions such as ABN AMRO, ANZ Bank, BNY Mellon, CLS Group, CME Group, the **Depository Trust and Clearing Corporation** (**DTCC**), Deutsche Börse Group, J.P. Morgan, State Street, SWIFT, and Wells Fargo
- Software companies such as SAP

- Academic institutions such as Cambridge Centre for Alternative Finance, blockchain at Columbia, and UCLA blockchain lab
- Systems integrators and other firms such as Accenture, Calastone, Wipro, Credits, Guardtime, IntellectEU, Nxt Foundation, and Symbiont

The evolution of blockchain

Blockchain technology is still at an early stage. It will take many years before it becomes mature and its potential is fully explored and harnessed. Currently, there is no universally agreed way to classify or define blockchain generation.

In her book on blockchain, Melanie Swan defined blockchain 1.0 to 3.0 based on the use scenarios that blockchain platforms are created to serve:

> *"Blockchain 1.0 is currency, the deployment of cryptocurrencies in applications related to cash, such as currency transfer, remittance, and digital payment systems.*
>
> *Blockchain 2.0 is contracts, the entire slate of economic, market, and financial applications using the blockchain that are more expensive than simple cash transactions: stocks, bonds, futures, loans, mortgages, titles, smart property, and smart contracts.*
>
> *Blockchain 3.0 is blockchain applications beyond currency, finance, and markets - particularly in the areas of government, health, science, literacy, culture, and art."*

Some others divided blockchain evolution into four generations from blockchain 1.0 to 4.0:

- **Blockchain 1.0**: With Bitcoin being the most prominent example in this segment, use cases were based on the **distributed ledger technology** (**DLT**) where financial transactions could be executed. Cryptocurrency was used as cash for the Internet.
- **Blockchain 2.0**: With Ethereum being the most prominent example in this segment, the new key concept was Smart Contracts, which are stored and executed on a blockchain.

- **Blockchain 3.0**: The keyword is DApps, an abbreviation for decentralized applications, which avoided centralized infrastructure. They use decentralized storage and decentralized communication. Unlike a smart contract which only involves a backend or server-side code, a DApp can have frontend code and user interfaces, i.e. client-side code to interact with its backend code on a blockchain. Like the smart contract code, a DApp's frontend can be stored and executed on decentralized storage such as Ethereums Swarm. In summary, a DApp is frontend plus contracts running on Ethereum.
- **Blockchain 4.0**: Blockchain platforms in this segment are built to serve for Industry 4.0. Industry 4.0 refers, in a simple way, to automation, enterprise resource planning, and integration of different execution systems.

Regardless of how the blockchain technology is divided into versions, it is certain that the technology growth is far from being over. New ideas and implementations will be incorporated into the existing platforms to deal with challenges for real-life problems. In other words, blockchain technology will be nimble and is self-adjusted to be an enabler in resolving business problems.

Summary

Blockchain is an emerging technology. Thanks to its immutability, transparency, the consensus mechanism for avoiding double spending, along with other clever designs such as blocks chained with the hashes of the previous blocks, the technology allows untrusting parties to trade with each other. In this chapter, we explained the basic concepts of its important features. Most of the discussions were about Bitcoin, which is the mother of the technology. We briefly talked about Ethereum, which extended Bitcoin and introduced the concept of smart contracts. The introduction of smart contracts makes the Ethereum blockchain generic and allows us to develop applications beyond the borderless cash payment use case for which Bitcoin was invented. The concept of an enterprise chain, along with one of the examples, Hyperledger, was mentioned as well. Finally, we briefly touched on the evolution of blockchain to give readers an idea of the trend in the technology. In the next chapter, we will discuss the concepts of Ethereum in detail.

2
Ethereum Fundamentals

Ethereum is an open source public blockchain and is considered to be an alternative coin to Bitcoin. A Canadian cryptocurrency researcher and programmer, Vitalik Buterin, proposed the idea in late 2013. Founded by an online crowdsale that took place in the middle of 2014, the platform went live at the end of July 2015. *The DAO* event in 2016 led to a hard fork, resulting in a split into **Ethereum** (**ETH**) and **Ethereum Classic** (**ETC**).

In this chapter, we cover the following topics about Ethereum:

- Overview of Ethereum
- Basic concepts such as ether, ERC20 tokens, smart contracts, EVM, gas, accounts, and oracles
- The Ethereum performance issue and ongoing efforts to address the issue, such as PoS, Casper, Plasma, and Sharding

An overview of Ethereum

In late 2013, Vitalik Buterin sent an email to the blockchain community announcing a white paper outlining the idea for Ethereum. He described it as a universal platform with internal languages, so anyone could write an application. According to Vitalik, the original idea for Ethereum was to create a general-purpose blockchain for fintech. Ethereum is a variation on Bitcoin. Unlike Bitcoin, which is a blockchain focusing on payments, Ethereum is a programmable, general-purpose blockchain. The introduction of smart contracts is the key to differentiating Ethereum from Bitcoin.

A well-known analogy to describe Ethereum and smart contracts, which bring together untrusting parties trading digital or digitized physical assets, is a vending machine, as described at the end of `Chapter 1`, *Introduction to Blockchain Technology*.

After a vending machine is made, nobody, including the machine owner, can change the rules. A buyer does not need to worry about the owner altering the rules prior to or during the transaction. As a result, a buyer can trust the machine to behave in the expected way and feels comfortable enough to go ahead with a transaction. Of course, the vending machine does not necessarily provide a perfect solution. A customer could occasionally face a malfunctioning machine and insert $1, yet nothing happens. If the vending machine does not provide a refund solution, such as posting a contact phone, the customer would permanently lose the $1. On the other hand, Ethereum's solution is much more robust. The rules in the form of smart contracts are distributed to all nodes. The same smart contracts will run on thousands of nodes (or even more) worldwide at approximately the same time. As long as at least one node runs, the transaction is successfully executed. In other words, Ethereum is truly a world computer.

Some blockchain enthusiasts responded to Vitalik's email and formed a core group in advancing and executing the idea. (This groundbreaking paper, titled *A Next-Generation Smart Contract and Decentralized Application Platform*, is available at `https://github.com/ethereum/wiki%20Wiki/`, archived from the original on 28 March 2015 with 169 revisions as of August 22, 2018.) In January 2014, the Ethereum Foundation was created. Soon (in early 2014), a British computer science PhD, Gavin Wood, published a yellow paper titled *Ethereum: A Secure Decentralized Generalized Transaction Ledger* (`https://ethereum.github.io/yellowpaper/paper.pdf`). Gavin's paper unified multiple initiatives for implementing the Ethereum idea and served as a blueprint for future development work.

Before talking about the Ethereum crowdsale event, we need to first explain the concept of **crowdfunding**. Crowdfunding refers to the practice of funding a project or an initiative by raising money from a large number of people, commonly on the internet. Crowdfunding is an alternative way of financing an initiative. In the case of blockchain projects, crowdfunding often takes place in the form of a project owner selling a portion of a hardcoded (preminted) total number of digital coins in circulation, exchanging them for an amount in a fiat currency or another established digital currency such as Bitcoin.

From July to August 2014, an online crowdfunding sale took place. The event led to selling 11.9 million coins of *premined* Ether—Ethereum's native cryptocurrency. This is about 12% of the total Ether coin supply: 102,431,467. Funded by the proceeds from this crowdfunding sale, development started. The core Ethereum team consisted of Vitalik Buterin, Mihai Alisie, Anthony Di Iorio, and Charles Hoskinson. The real development of the Ethereum project was started by a Swiss company, Ethereum Switzerland GmbH (EthSuisse). The platform went live on 30 July 2015.

Stephan Tual, an ex-Ethereum CMO, formed a company called the *The DAO* on April 30, 2016. The purpose of this entity was to manage the process of selecting which smart contract to deploy. *The DAO* came up with the clever idea of selecting contracts based on investments. Completed smart contracts were posted on the internet. A potential investor would declare an amount to be invested in a smart contract. Smart contracts with the top amounts would be chosen for deployment. *The DAO* raised a record US $150 million via crowdfunding sales to fund the project. *The DAO* was hacked in June and lost US $50 million worth of Ether due to bugs in its software. The hacking ignited a heated debate within the Ethereum community on how to deal with it. Two contesting opinions emerged:

- Enhance the Ethereum code to make a similar attack in future not feasible and deploy the code to all nodes
- Make no changes to the core Ethereum code and take the risk of future attacks

Vitalik made a call for a hard fork solution and publicly asked all Ethereum nodes to stop trading for the deployment of patch code. Within hours, all of the thousands of nodes worldwide were completely shut down. The majority of the nodes voted for adopting the hard fork approach and upgraded their core Ethereum code with the patch, yet a small portion of nodes chose not to take the patch and still run the same code.

This hard fork event split the Ethereum blockchain into two. The nodes running the old code maintaining the original blockchain became Ethereum Classic, with the coin symbol ETC, and the nodes with the patched code, maintaining a forked Ethereum blockchain, became Ethereum, with the coin symbol ETH. The fork occurred exactly at block number 1,920,000. The hard fork created a rivalry between the two networks. Now, the ETH price has gone up more than 130 times and ETC is worth only one-tenth of ETH's price, due to its unpopularity and the concerns of suffering a future *The DAO* type of attack.

After the *The DAO* hard fork, Ethereum forked twice in Q4 of 2016 to deal with new attacks. While the hard forks resolved past hackers' attacks, this is obviously not a scalable solution as one cannot always rely on creating a hard fork to resolve every future hack. Consequently, Ethereum has increased its protection by preventing new spam attacks by hackers.

While hard forks are used to address hacking, soft forks are used by Ethereum for protocol upgrades, which are important changes affecting the underlying functionality and/or incentive structures of Ethereum. Some notable soft forks are as follows:

- **Homestead** was for improvements to transaction processing, gas pricing, and security. The soft fork took place on 31 July 2015.
- **Metropolis part 1**: **Byzantium** was for changes to reduce the complexity of the EVM and add more flexibility for smart contract developers. The soft fork took place on 16 October 2017.
- Two more protocol upgrades are planned in the future: **Metropolis part 2**: *Constantinople* helps to lay the foundations for the transition to proof-of-stake.

In March 2017, blockchain startups, research groups, and major companies created the **Enterprise Ethereum Alliance** (**EEA**) consisting of 30 founding members. In May, the nonprofit organization expanded to include 16 enterprise members with household names such as Cornell University's research group, Samsung SDS, Microsoft, Intel, J. P. Morgan, DTCC, Deloitte, Accenture, Banco Santander, BNY Mellon, ING, and National Bank of Canada. By July 2017, the list had increased to 159 members.

Despite the many improvements made since its initial launch, Ethereum continues to evolve. Ethereum 2.0 sets out to address one of the weakest links, scalability, and is expected to launch in 2019, in phases, as per Vitalik's recent comments.

Ethereum basic concepts

Ethereum builds on top of the Bitcoin blockchain, including key features such as a distributed ledger containing chained blocks, the proof-of-work algorithm, and so on. However, its biggest addition is the introduction of smart contracts, which are coded in a Turing-complete scripting language. Because of this new addition, unlike Bitcoin or its non-smart contract close relatives, Ethereum allows developers to address generic business problems.

Before getting to the basic concepts, we summarize some useful facts on Ethereum as follows:

- Ethereum has three main ingredients:
    - **Decentralization**: For guaranteed execution
    - **Hashes**: For safeguarding the world state
    - **Signatures**: For authorizing programs and transactions

- Since Ethereum is a blockchain, it uses mathematical algorithms to replace intermediary entities and bring untrusting parties together to do businesses.
- Ethereum blockchain brings trust in data due to its ability to verify the validity of data on a node via its consensus mechanism.
- It uses total validation to replace central control.
- Like a transaction, a digital signature is required for deploying a smart contract. A deployed smart contract is permanent and is immutable.
- A smart contract is assigned with an address.
- Suppose a smart contract has a bug and requires a fix. The patched smart contract will be deployed with a newly assigned address and therefore is treated as a completely new smart contract with no relationship to the old one.
- In May 2017, Ethereum had 25,000 reachable nodes worldwide, consisting of full nodes and light nodes.
- A full node has the full blockchain downloaded and available. The Ethereum ledger can be pruned. Full nodes verify transactions in a block in construction. A miner node has to be a full node.
- A light node does not store the entire blockchain, but it stores the parts it cares about from someone it trusts.
- Scripts of a contract code are executed via the **Ethereum virtual machine** (**EVM**) on full nodes. A smart contract's address stores bytecode, called opcode, that runs on the EVM.
- Since a smart contract runs on full nodes on tens of thousands of machines, it truly is worldwide. In other words, writing a smart contract to a blockchain is global and permanent.
- Since smart contract scripts are stored in a decentralized way, it provides an additional layer of security. This is true as all full nodes know that other nodes store the same code. It is not feasible for a hacker to push malicious scripts to all good nodes worldwide and crash them.
- A smart contract is a scripted legal document and is guaranteed for execution. Since a smart contract is signed at its deployment and a transaction that invokes it is also signed, there should not be a dispute between the two trading parties in the transaction. In other words, with a decentralized blockchain such as Ethereum, the need for a judge disappears! node and can grow to a full network.
- Thanks to the nature of permanence and immutability, data and programs on Ethereum blockchain are auditable. This could be of special interest to the government for enforcing regulation and compliance requirements.
- Ethereum is open source. Anyone can download the code and create his or her own version of an Ethereum network. Of course, the issue is about how to convince others of its value so they join the network.

- Ethereum is decentralized. As a result, there is no master node that controls or dictates the whole network. The network operates via consensus, as per its protocols.
- Ethereum provides fault tolerance as well. As long as at least one full node survives during a catastrophic attack, the network can be rebuilt from the surviving node and grow to a full network.
- While Ethereum provides extreme robustness, the flip side is the problem of how to stop it when it is out of control. Like in the example of the *The DAO* hack, the network had to rely on Vitalik and his authority to shut it down completely. Compared to today, the network then was many times smaller. As the network continues to grow in size, this approach will become harder. In future, the network may grow to tens of millions of nodes or more. As long as one node does not respond to an authoritative call, the Ethereum network is still alive. In other words, it becomes extremely difficult to shut down a network completely. Of course, this is what a decentralized blockchain is all about: no centralized authority dictating to everyone else!
- Ethereum allows for recursive calls to other smart contracts. Poorly written smart contracts can lead to infinite loops. To address this issue, Ethereum builds in a circuit breaker mechanism, Gas, which is explained later in detail.
- On a big data platform, a task is divided into chunks that are distributed to nodes on the network and the work is shared by nodes. However, Ethereum's full nodes execute the same pieces of scripts. That means every full node of the Ethereum blockchain stores and computes the same data; this is reliable but not scalable. The scalability issue is one of the major criticisms of Ethereum. As we will discuss later, multiple efforts are underway to address this issue.
- Ether is the native cryptocurrency of Ethereum. Ethereum allows a user to issue their own digital coins called tokens. ERC-20/ERC-721/ERC 1400 are common technical standards to be followed for issuing Ethereum tokens.
- Ethereum can be seen as the third generation of the internet. This could be one reason that Ethereum's JS API was called Web3. There are discussions on rewriting the internet with blockchain technology.
- The practice of providing centralized services on top of a decentralized internet (such as Google providing a centralized searching functionality on a decentralized internet) will apply to blockchain as well.

Ether

Since Ethereum is built on top of Bitcoin, it is considered to be a Bitcoin altcoin. Ether to Ethereum is similar to BTC to Bitcoin. Ethereum is the name used when referring to the protocols, the blockchain, the client software, and the mainnet.

The Ethereum mainnet is the blockchain network that is used by clients for transferring a digital asset from a sender to a recipient. In other words, it is the network where actual transactions take place on a distributed ledger. Mainnet is equivalent to a production environment. The Ethereum testnet is for development. As mentioned at `https://www.ethernodes.org/network/2`, as of October 8, 2018, the mainnet had 13,662 nodes and the testnet had 29 nodes. Since the actual transactions take place on the mainnet, Ether has a real value only on the Ethereum mainnet. In other words, on the testnet, it is worth nothing. Ether coins (ETH and ETC) are listed and exchanged in tens of thousands of digital currency markets. Their prices vary greatly. For example, on October 8, 2018, ETH was traded at around $223 and ETC at $11.

Ether can be transferred between addresses (accounts). It is used to pay miners for their computational work; they are paid in transaction fees and also for gas consumption resulting from executing a transaction. Here, the concept of gas is essential for Ethereum and it is discussed later in more detail.

Ether is the largest denomination. There are other units. The smallest is called WEI, named after the digital money pioneer, Wei Dai, who is the inventor of B-money. B-money was his proposal for an anonymous, distributed electronic cash system. Other units include Gwei, microether, and milliether. They all have a second name. For example, milliether is also called finney, named after another digital money pioneer, Harold Thomas Finney II, who in 2004 wrote the world's first implemented cryptocurrency, RPOW (reusable proofs of work) before Bitcoin. The following table gives the conversion rate between ether and other units:

Unit	Wei value	Wei
Gwei (shannon)	10^9 Wei	1,000,000,000
microether (szabo)	10^{12} Wei	1,000,000,000,000
miliether (finney)	10^{15} Wei	1,000,000,000,000,000
ether	10^{18} Wei	1,000,000,000,000,000,000

ERC20 tokens

Ethereum is a generic blockchain. It allows developers to build a DApp and trade digital assets. Correspondingly, it allows a developer to define a user-specific coin called a token. The majority of these tokens are ERC20 tokens. ERC refers to Ethereum Request for Comment, and 20 is the number that was assigned to this request. In other words, ERC-20 is a technical standard used for smart contracts on the Ethereum blockchain for implementing tokens. According to Etherscan.io, as of October 8, 2018, a total of 125,330 ERC-20 compatible tokens were found on the Ethereum main network.

ERC-20 defines a list of rules for Ethereum tokens to follow. By doing so, it allows for interaction and conversion between Ethereum tokens within the larger Ethereum ecosystem. Currently, Ether does not conform to the ERC-20 standard. However, since Ether is the native coin of Ethereum, it can be converted into other tokens. The ERC-20 specification defines an interface containing methods and events.

The following is list of required methods (github.com):

- `name`: It returns the name of the token, for instance, `HelloToken: function name() view returns (string name)`.
- `symbol`: It returns the symbol of the token, for instance, `HTC: function symbol() view returns (string symbol)`.
- `decimals`: It returns the number of decimals the token uses; for instance, 8 means to divide the token amount by 100,000,000 to get its user representation: `function decimals() view returns (uint8 decimals)`.
- `totalSupply`: It returns the total token supply: `function totalSupply() view returns (uint256 totalSupply)`.
- `balanceOf`: It returns the account balance of another account with `address _owner: function balanceOf (address _owner) view returns (uint256 balance)`.
- `transfer`: It transfers a specified number (`_value`) of tokens to the `_to` address, and MUST fire the transfer event. The function should throw an error if the `_from` account balance does not have enough tokens to spend: `function transfer(address _to, uint256 _value) returns (bool success)`.
- `transferFrom`: It transfers a specified amount (`_value`) of tokens from the `_from` address to the `_to` address, and MUST fire the Transfer event. The function should throw an error unless the `_from` account has deliberately authorized the sender of the message via some mechanism: `function transferFrom (address _from, address _to, uint256 _value) returns (bool success)`.

- `approve`: It allows `_spender` to withdraw from your account multiple times, up to the `_value` amount. If this function is called again, it overwrites the current allowance with `_value: function approve (address _spender, uint256 _value) returns (bool success)`.
- `allowance`: It returns the amount that `_spender` is still allowed to withdraw from `_owner: function allowance (address _owner, address _spender) view returns (uint256 remaining)`.

The list of required events is as follows:

- `transfer`: Must trigger when tokens are transferred, including zero value transfers. A token contract that creates new tokens SHOULD trigger a `Transfer` event with the `_from` address set to 0x0 when tokens are created: `event Transfer (address indexed _from, address indexed _to, uint256 _value)`.
- `approval`: Must trigger on any successful call to approve `(address _spender, uint256 _value): event Approval (address indexed _owner, address indexed _spender, uint256 _value)`.

Although Ethereum allows for a person to create his or her own money, Ethereum's true value is its guaranteed execution of a smart contract. Ether and ERC20 token creation are mainly for initial crowdfunding purposes to support a project and are used for payment during the transaction to circumvent a bank. Without a real business use case, a token is worth nothing.

Smart contracts

The term *smart contract* was initially coined by Nick Szabo, who is a computer scientist, a legal scholar, and the inventor of Bit Gold, in 1994. He is a living legend in the world of cryptocurrency for his research into digital contracts and digital currency. He is even considered to be Satoshi Nakomoto by some people, although he rejected that claim.

Nick Szabo originally defined smart contracts as follows:

> *"A smart contract is a computerized transaction protocol that executes the terms of a contract. The general objectives of smart contract design are to satisfy common contractual conditions (such as payment terms, liens, confidentiality, and even enforcement), minimize exceptions both malicious and accidental, and minimize the need for trusted intermediaries. Related economic goals include lowering fraud loss, arbitration and enforcement costs, and other transaction costs."*

With a vending machine, transaction rules are built into the machine hardware. Transaction rules on a digital asset are built into scripts. That is, the smart contract consists of code. Here are some useful facts on smart contracts:

- A smart contract is immutable.
- A smart contract is permanent.
- A smart contract is timestamped.
- A smart contract is globally available.
- A smart contract is a digitized legal document.
- A smart contract is a computer protocol intended to facilitate, verify, or enforce an agreed contract between trading parties digitally.
- Smart contracts allow for execution of transactions without the third party as an intermediary. The transactions are auditable and irreversible.
- A smart contract moves digital coins, executes a conventional payment, or transfers a digital asset, or even delivers real-world goods and services.
- For a third-party-involved business transaction, for instance, buying/selling a house, escrow accounts are often used to temporarily store the trading parties' money. With a smart contract, no escrow account is needed. Smart contracts eliminate the need for escrow accounts since they are guaranteed to be executed for transferring the money and assets.
- Smart contracts provide more security than traditional contract law and their transaction costs are only a fraction of other transaction costs associated with contracting.
- In the interpretation used by the Ethereum Foundation, a smart contract does not necessarily refer to the classical concept of a contract. It can be any kind of computer program.
- To deploy and run a smart contract, one has to digitally sign the deployment, similar to sending other data or transactions on the Ethereum blockchain.
- Smart contracts can be public and are open to developers. This leads to a security issue. If a smart contract has a bug or security loophole, it is visible to all developers. To make the issue worse, such a bug or loophole is not easily fixable, due to its immutability. This gives hackers plenty of time to explore weaknesses and initiate attacks on the Ethereum blockchain. *The DAO* event was a high-profile example of this issue.

An Ethereum smart contract can be developed in one of four languages: solidity (inspired by JavaScript), Serpent (inspired by Python, no longer used), LLL (inspired by Lisp), and Mutan (inspired by Go, no longer used). Regardless of the language used, smart contracts are coded in a high-level programming language which needs to be compiled into a low level, machine-runnable language. In the Ethereum smart contract implementation, a VM approach similar to the concept of Java VM (JVM) is used. The Ethereum VM is called **EVM.** Smart contract scripts are converted to EVM-runnable code called **bytecode**. The opcode is then deployed to the Ethereum blockchain for execution. Currently, a research-oriented language is under development, which is called Vyper and is a strongly typed Python-based language.

Ethereum virtual machines

In the sixties, when computers had just been invented, coding was in a lower level language, for instance an assembly language (assembler). For example, an assembler code line, *ADD R1 R2 R3,* is an instruction to add the contents of register 1 and register 2 with the result being placed in the third register, R3. A register is a temporary storage area built into a CPU. With a 32-bit CPU, a register is 32 bits long.

The code in an assembly language is then converted to a machine language in 0 and 1 sequences, which is machine-executable. Coding in a low-level language is tedious and time-consuming. When high-level languages such as ALGOL or BASIC were invented, coding time was greatly reduced. However, the underlying process remained the same: compiling the code into a machine executable language in 0 and 1 sequences. Java, Python, JavaScript and C++ are currently popular high-level languages.

While the compiling approach works well, it does have one inconvenience: lack of portability. A piece of code that is compiled on a computer is machine-dependent. In other words, it is not portable. To address this issue, the concept of the virtual machine was introduced. A **virtual machine** (**VM**) is an emulation of a computer system. There are two types of virtual machine: **system virtual machine** (also called full virtualization), which provide a substitute for a real machine, and **process virtual machines,** which are for executing computer programs in a platform-independent environment. It is the process of VM that we refer to in our preceding discussion.

A program written in a high-level language is compiled into VM-executable code. As long as a computer supports such a VM, the compiled code can run on it without the need to be recompiled. For example, JVM is a well-known Java VM that enables a computer to run Java programs compiled into Java bytecode.

In the case of Ethereum, smart contracts are written in a high-level language, mostly solidity. A smart contract is compiled to opcodes, which are executable on a VM built specifically for Ethereum, the **EVM**. The EVM brings portability along with robustness, since EVM performs runtime checks to prevent crashes. These types of checks do have a performance penalty though.

Since Ethereum contracts can be written in any one of the four languages: solidity, serpent, LLL, and Mutan, there are four compilers to convert each of the four languages' coded smart contracts into opcodes for running on the EVM. Another relevant concept is the **Ethereum client**, which refers to a collection of software being installed on a node for parsing and verifying blockchain transactions, smart contracts, and everything related. The Ethereum client is implemented in one of eight languages: Python, C++, Go, JavaScript, Java, Haskell, Ruby, and Rust. Implemented EVMs are an essential part of the Ethereum client. As a result, opcodes can run on any one of the eight client implementations. EVM was originally designed for currency transactions and later extended to other digital assets. As a result, there are restrictions on supporting certain features. Developers face some severe restrictions (for instance, the use of string or local registers).

Ethereum gas

An Ethereum transaction can call a smart contract, which can in turn call another smart contract, and then another, and so on. When smart contracts are buggy, it can lead to infinite loops. Outside a blockchain, it is easy to resolve an infinite loop issue. One can stop the out-of-control program by simply shutting down a server, rebooting it, debugging the program, fixing the faulty logic in the code, recompiling it, and redeploying.

With the Ethereum blockchain, this approach simply does not work! Imagine if tens of thousands of nodes went into infinite loops at approximately the same time worldwide. In order to stop infinitely looping smart contracts, all the nodes need to be shut down within a short time window. As long as one node fails to comply, the infinitely looping smart contract would still be alive and running. It is a logistical nightmare to coordinate and shutdown all these nodes.

To resolve this issue, the concept of **gas** was introduced. A vehicle relies on an engine burning gas to move. When an engine runs out of gas, the vehicle stops. Ethereum introduced the gas concept to achieve the same effect. When submitting a transaction to the Ethereum blockchain, the requester is required to provide a max gas amount. For example, in the following example, a transaction request is submitted to call a **HelloWorld** smart contract with the maximum consumption not exceeding a specified gas value:

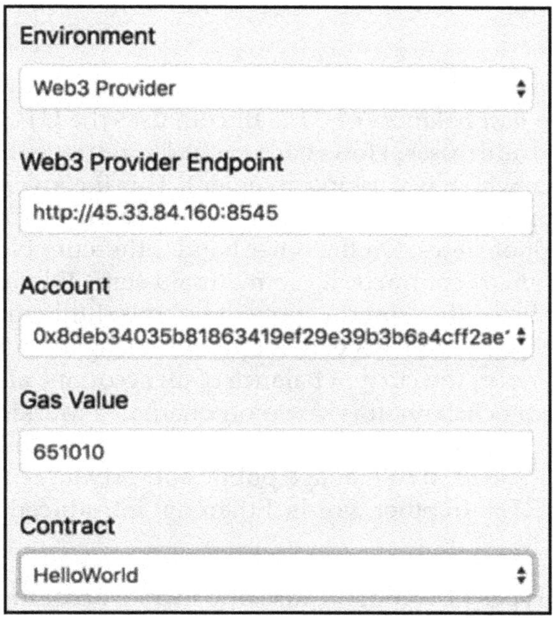

When this request is validated by mining nodes, the **HelloWorld** smart contract is invoked. Every operation running on the EVM consumes a predefined quantity of gas. For example, ADD (sum operation) consumes three gas and MUL (multiplication operation) uses five gas. For illustration purposes, suppose a smart contract was badly written and contains an infinite loop. Furthermore, we assume each loop consists of an ADD operation and a MUL operation. Therefore, a loop will consumes eight gas (three gas for ADD and five gas for MUL). After EVM executes enough loops, the specified maximum gas value will be consumed. Consequently, EVM stops executing the contract. Therefore, all nodes would stop running at approximately the same time. Another advantage of gas is to make spamming monetarily expensive and, therefore, reduce the risk of hacking.

Gas is a metering unit for measuring consumption, just as the kilowatt is the unit for measuring electricity usage. Suppose that, in a month, a family uses 210 KW. Before sending a bill to the family, the utility company first converts 210 KW into USD, based on a predefined conversion rate. Suppose a unit of KW costs $0.2 USD, the total charge for the month is 0.2 * 210 = $42 USD. Similarly, gas usage is converted to Ether and charged to a requester. Ethereum allows a requester to specify the conversion rate when the transaction is submitted. A miner has the right to selectively process transactions by giving higher priority to transactions with higher rates. If a requester does not specify a rate, EVM uses a default rate, which varies. For example, in 2016 the rate was 1 gas = 0.00001 ETH. In 2018, one gas = 0.00000002 ETH.

Account

In `Chapter 1`, *Introduction to Blockchain Technology*, we discussed addresses, an account-like concept, which is used to *host* balances of BTC. Bitcoin uses the UTOX model to manage the transfer of BTCs between addresses. However, one has to retrieve the entire ledger to find the balance of an address, which is very inconvenient. This inconvenience is due to the fact that Bitcoin does not support an on-chain Turing-complete programming language and it does not have the concept of states. On the other hand, Ethereum blockchain supports scripting languages and smart contracts; it can maintain state. Ethereum transactions manage state transitions by calling smart contract methods. Ethereum no longer needs to rely on UTOX to manage payments. Instead, it operates using accounts and balances via state transitions. State denotes the current balance of all accounts, along with other data. State is not stored on the blockchain. It is saved off-chain in a Merkle Patricia tree. This is because state is mutable data, while a block is not mutable. As with Bitcoin, a cryptocurrency wallet can be used to manage public and private *keys* or accounts, which are for receiving or sending ETH. In other words, Ethereum introduced the concept of **accounts**.

Ethereum supports two types of account: externally owned accounts (controlled by human users via ownership of private keys) and contract accounts.

- **An externally controlled account**:
    - Has an Ether balance
    - Can initiate transactions for either transferring Ether or triggering smart contract code
    - Is controlled by users via private keys
    - Has no associated smart contract code
- **A contract account**:
    - Has an Ether balance
    - Has associated smart contract code
    - Smart contract code execution is triggered by transactions or calls received from other contracts
- **For both types of account, there are four components**:
    - `nonce`: For an externally owned account, it refers to the number of transactions sent from the account's address; for a contract account, nonce is increased every time this contracts calls another contract
    - `balance`: It is the number of Wei owned by this address

- `storageRoot`: A 256-bit hash of the storage contents of the account
- `codeHash`: The hash of the code of this account is EVM; this is the code that gets executed when the address receives a call

When Ether is transferred from contract accounts to an externally owned account, there is a fee, for instance 21,000 gas. When Ether is sent from an externally owned account to a contract account, the fee is higher, and depends on the smart contract code and data being sent in the transaction.

Ethereum addresses have the following format:

1. Start with the prefix 0x, a common identifier for hexadecimal
2. Rightmost 20 bytes of the Keccak-256 hash (big-endian) of the ECDSA public key

Since, in hexadecimal, two digits are stored in one byte, a 20-byte address is represented with 40 hexadecimal digits. A sample address is `0xe99356bde974bbe08721d77712168fa074279267`.

Oracle

As we already learned, identical Ethereum smart contracts are executed on nodes worldwide. What we have not emphasized yet is that all these nodes take the same set of inputs and should yield the same outputs. This is called **determinism**. Ethereum relies on this determinism since, in order to verify the validity of smart contracts and transactions, mining nodes have to yield the same results while running the same code with the same inputs.

This determinism raises a challenge. On one side, Ethereum is a generic platform that can be used to transfer any digital or digitized assets. Its smart contracts require data or inputs from external sources such as the internet, for example, stock prices, macroeconomic or microeconomic indices, and so on. Without access to these sources of information, use cases for smart contracts will be restricted to only a tiny fraction of their potential. On the other side, even with a tiny time difference, nodes may retrieve different information from an external source. With different inputs, nodes will end up with different outputs. Consequently, the determinism property does not hold. As a result, smart contracts are not permitted to call an internet URL or directly pull data from an external source. To address the paradox, the concept of the **oracle** is implemented.

According to Merriam-Webster, one of the definitions of oracle is *a shrine in which a deity reveals hidden knowledge or the divine purpose through such a person*. In the blockchain world, an oracle refers to the third-party or decentralized data feed services that provide external data. Oracles provide interfaces from the real world to the digital world. Oracle data is not part of the blockchain. It is saved off-chain.

There are different types of oracle. Two of them are software oracles and hardware oracles:

- **Software oracles**: Normally refer to easily accessible online information such as stock index close prices, FX rates, economic news or weather forecasts, and so on. Software oracles are useful since they provide smart contracts with wide varieties and up-to-date information.
- **Hardware oracles**: Normally refers to scanned information such as UPS delivery scanning, registered mail scanning, or supplier goods delivery scanning. This feed can be useful to activate a smart contract that is triggered upon an event's occurrence.

Other concepts

Since Ethereum is built on top of Bitcoin, many of the basic concepts were already discussed in `Chapter 1`, *Introduction to Blockchain Technology*. For the rest of this subsection, we briefly cover a few of them with a focus on the key differences.

- **Consensus algorithms**:
    - Like Bitcoin, PoW is its consensus algorithm. Unlike Bitcoin, Ethereum is working on switching to another consensus algorithm called **Proof-of-Stake** (**PoS**) to significantly improve performance with its next release tag of serenity.
- **Private blockchain**:
    - In general, both Bitcoin and Ethereum are public blockchains since the network is open to anyone and a node can join freely.
    - Ethereum has variants on private chains. With private Ethereum, a node needs approval prior to joining a network. These blockchains are called private blockchains. Private blockchains are suitable for enterprise applications. Hyperledger and JPM Morgan's Quorum are examples of well-known private blockchain variants of Ethereum. Another example is Brainbot's hydrachain.

- **Off-chain data**:
    - With the Bitcoin blockchain, we do not talk much about the concept of off-chain data. With the Ethereum blockchain, this topic needs to be discussed. There are multiple scenarios where data cannot be stored on-chain:
        - The first case is state variables. All data stored in a blockchain is immutable since the contents of a block are hashed and blocks are linked via these hashes. A tiny change in the contents of a block will lead to the reconstruction of all the blocks afterwards, which is obviously not feasible. However, state variables are, for instance, used to hold balances. They do change content to reflect the balance move. A solution is to save them off-chain.
        - Oracles are another example, where information pulled from external sources is saved off-chain to be fed to smart contracts.
        - Ethereum was invented to allow for trading generic digital or digitized assets. Metadata describing the underlying assets is saved off-chain.
        - With Bitcoin, the distributed ledger has to be saved on all nodes in order to provide the information required for transaction validation. In the case of Ethereum, the balance of a cryptocurrency or digital asset can be directly retrieved from state variables. There is no need to browse the ledger to obtain balances in order to determine whether a _from address has sufficient funds. As a result, a full node can choose to keep only a portion of the ledger, that is, trim a ledger. The blocks being trimmed can be saved off-chain at a centralized location for future inquiries.

- **Testing**:
    - It is vital to thoroughly test, double-test, and triple-test a smart contract. Safety testing is critical. As explained earlier, in Ethereum's short history, there have been several high-profile hacking events, which occurred mainly due to buggy smart contract code.
    - Ethereum is less safe than Bitcoin because of bugs introduced in smart contracts. Ethereum smart contracts are saved in chained blocks and are not encrypted. Hackers can easily spot and explore the vulnerability of buggy contract code and engage in attacks. On the other hand, like Bitcoin, data and transactions on Ethereum are relatively secure and not vulnerable to hacking. It is only the contract that a hacker can construct malicious transactions to call and abuse.
    - After a smart contract is deployed, it is permanent and immutable. Deployment of revised code will become a new contract with a different address. It has different state variables with new balances.
    - Deployment of a smart contract is not free. It burns gas.
- **Digital signature, encryption, and public/private keys**:
    - Bitcoin is a multi-signature process. In order for a transaction to be executed, both sides have to sign it. Ethereum is similar. In addition, deployment of a smart contract also requires digital signatures.
    - Like Bitcoin, with an Ethereum blockchain one can take a wallet application and generate a pair of public and private keys at the same time. An address is derived from a public key; that is, an address is just the hash of a public key. A sender uses a private key to sign a transaction and a receiver uses a public key to verify the authenticity of a signature. In general, a pair of public and private keys can be used to support the following two types of activity:
    - **Sending a secret message**: The public key is used to encrypt a message and the private key is used to decrypt the message.
    - **Signature**: A private key is used to encrypt and generate a signature. The public key is used to decrypt for signature verification.
    - Block transaction contents in both Bitcoin and Ethereum are currently not encrypted. On the other hand, block contents in Zcash are encrypted.

  - Since every Ethereum transaction, including smart contracts, has to be digitally signed, a node only needs to accept digitally signed requests, potentially without the need to verify the entire transaction history. This approach can help to improve performance.
- **DAO**:
  - DAO refers to a decentralized autonomous organization. One should not confuse it with the organization called *The DAO*, which is famously linked to a hacking event that resulted in the split of **Ethereum** into **Ethereum** (**ETH**) and **Ethereum Classic** (**ETC**).
  - DAO can be considered to consist of smart contracts, which is in term-built form decentralized codes, that is, a hierarchical structure of decentralized core → smart contract → DAO.
    - Decentralized code is saved in multiple nodes. It will definitely run and cannot be stopped.
    - Smart contracts move money and digital assets.
    - DAO consists of smart contracts and creates an independent entity or community.
- **DApp**:
  - DApp is a big topic. We briefly mention it due to restrictions on the size of the book:
    - DApp refers to decentralized application and uses decentralized code.
    - Ethereum is a general-purpose DApp platform.
    - An Ethereum DApp, like any other blockchain DApp, has a decentralized backend (for instance, smart contracts) and a centralized frontend (a client-side application for interacting with the blockchain). This architecture is due to the performance and limitations of today's blockchain.
    - As discussed before, a large portion of the backend, the database and business logic, is hosted off-ch.

- **Ethereum issues**:
    - Ethereum suffers from issues inherited from Bitcoin:
        - Data can get lost due to forking or splitting. When there are two competing chains, the chain that cannot manage to grow fast has to be discarded in order to maintain data consistency on all nodes. Transactions on the short chain will get lost if they are not included in blocks of the winning chain without even being known by their original requesters!
        - Since data on-chain is not encrypted, a blockchain is not anonymous and not confidential.
        - Addresses are not verified. This is bad. When a receiver's address is wrongly entered, the coins being transferred to it will be permanent as transactions are permanent and coins are locked forever!
        - The PoW algorithm consumes a huge amount of power. It is reported that some large mining operations in China require dedicated power stations to supply electricity.

Performance

Another problem inherited from Bitcoin is that Ethereum is slow. It is many magnitudes slower than other platforms that host transaction data, for instance a traditional database. For example, it takes an average of 10 minutes to build a new record for Bitcoin. As a rule of thumb, after waiting for six new blocks to be built, a transaction is considered to be finalized (the same as a commitment in a database). This means that, on average, a requester will wait for one hour to see a request completed. In Ethereum, the average time for miners to build a block is 17 seconds and it is recommended you wait for 12 blocks before a transaction is confirmed. This is 12 * 17 = 204 seconds, or 3.4 minutes' waiting time for a user. Here, waiting for a few subsequent blocks to be built before confirming a transaction is useful. At any point, Ethereum can have competing chains. The waiting gives Ethereum sufficient time to work out the issue of having competing chains and reach a consensus.

Throughput

Throughput is a measure of how many units of information a system can process in a given time window. To measure performance on a transaction platform, throughput is expressed in terms of **TPS**, transactions per second:

- For Bitcoin, TPS can be computed as follows. A Bitcoin block normally contains 1,500-2,000 transactions. Let's use the high-end number, 2,000. Since it takes 60 minutes to confirm these 2000 transactions, its TPS = 2,000 / (60*60) = 0.56; that is, only half a transaction per second. A similar calculation for Ethereum yields a TPS = 2,000 / 204 = 9.8, almost 10 transactions per second—much better than Bitcoin. Led by Vitalik, the Ethereum Foundation is working on the sharding approach, targeting at increasing TPS by 80 times.
- For comparison, VISA has an average TPS of 2000 with a peak at 40,000. A high-performance database such as VoltDB can handle over a million insertions per second. A stock exchange can match thousands of trades per second.
- However, this comparison is not complete. From a business point of view, a credit card or exchange transaction is finalized only when it is cleared and settled. For credit cards, a billing cycle is normally 2-3 months. A stock exchange takes three days to settle a transaction. In this sense, Ethereum is much faster, since on the blockchain transaction and settlement occur simultaneously.
- When compared with a database, Ethereum is at a disadvantage. A database commitment can take place right after the insertion, updating, or deletion of a transaction.
- These are the reasons causing Ethereum's slowness:
    - Every full node must execute the same smart contract code.
    - As the Ethereum network becomes larger, the time for reaching a consensus will take longer, as it takes time to transfer data between a growing number of nodes to verify transactions, access info, and communicate.
- There are ways to increase the throughput. The following are a few:
    - When the block size is increased, more transactions can be hosted in a block and a higher TPS can be obtained.
    - Running multiple chains in parallel. Enterprise chains such as Hyperledger Fabric and R3's Corda use this approach.

- State channel design helps to increase throughput. An example of a state channel implementation for Ethereum is Raiden. Micro Raiden was launched in November 2017. The idea behind state channels is to use off-chain for a transaction between two parties and use on-chain for the settlement of the transaction. Off-chain transactions are another topic worth an in-depth discussion, but not in this book.

Proof-of-Stake (PoS)

The PoS consensus algorithm is based on the principle that when a miner owns more coins, the miner has more power to mine or validate transactions, a higher chance of building new blocks, and therefore a higher chance of receiving more reward coins. PoS is energy-efficient and can reach a consensus much faster.

Several randomization methods are available for selecting a miner to build the next block, not just based on Ether balances of externally owned accounts, in order to avoid a scenario where the richest miner is always selected:

- **Randomized block selection**: Uses a formula to look for the lowest hash value in combination with the size of the stake for selecting a miner.
- **Coin age-based selection**: Coins owned for long enough, say 30 days, are eligible to compete for the next block. A miner with older and larger sets of coins has a better chance of being granted the role.
- **Delegated Proof-of-Stake**: This implementation chooses a limited number of nodes to propose and validate blocks to the blockchain.
- **Randomized Proof-of-Stake**: Each node is selected randomly, using a verifiable random beacon to build the new block.

Ethereum is working on replacing PoW with PoS in a new tagged release.

Casper

PoS is being worked on as a replacement to the computationally inefficient PoW algorithm. PoS is not being fully implemented and upgraded on mainnet due to concerns about an issue such as emerging of a set of centralized supernodes (which receive an outsized role in building the new blocks). Casper is the Ethereum community's effort to transition from PoW to PoS.

In the Per Casper protocol, validators (the Ethereum equivalent of miners in Bitcoin) set aside a portion of their Ether as a stake. When a validator identifies a candidate block to build, Ether is bet on that block by the validator. If the block is indeed added to the chain, the validator is rewarded based on the size of his or her bet. Validators acting maliciously will be penalized by having their stakes removed. Casper has two main projects: Casper FFG and Casper CCB.

Casper FFG (Friendly Finality Gadget; Vitalik's version of Casper) is a hybrid algorithm running on PoW but treating every 50th block on the network as a PoS checkpoint. Validators vote on the finality of these blocks and write them into the blockchain. FFG is meant to be an intermediate step in a transition to a complete adoption of PoS. FFG is already running on a test network. It will soon be implemented completely on mainnet. The Casper **CBC** (**Correct by Construction**, Vlad's Casper) is more dramatic. CBC focuses on designing protocols where one can extend local views of a node's estimate of safety to achieve consensus safety. So far, the approach has been merely researched and no release plan is available for making it to Ethereum.

Plasma

In 2017, Buterin and Joseph Poon presented their idea, which called for scaling up Ethereum's performance, that is, increasing TPS. Like the state channel design, plasma is a technique for conducting off-chain transactions while relying on the underlying Ethereum blockchain to provide its security. Therefore, plasma belongs to the group of *off-chain* technologies. Truebit is another example in this group.

Plasma works as follows:

- Smart contracts are created on the main-chain and served to be the roots for Plasma child-chains. They define rules for child chains and are called to move assets between the main-chain and child-chains.
- A child-chain is created with its own consensus algorithm, for instance, PoS.
- Deploy smart contracts, which define the actual business rules, to the child-chain.
- Digital assets being created on the main-chain are transferred onto the child-chain by calling the plasma rooting contracts.
- The block builders on the child-chain periodically commit a validation to the main-chain, proving that the current state of the child-chain is valid, in accordance with the consensus rules. A user sends and gets requests executed without ever interacting with the main-chain directly.

Plasma has these advantages:

- Allows an Ethereum blockchain to handle larger datasets
- Enables more complicated applications to run on the blockchain
- Increases throughput greatly

The Ethereum community is actively working on the implementation of Ethereum plasma. Plasma-MVP (minimum viable product) is being worked on first, to gain experience and test its viability. There is the possibility of releasing plasma-mvp by the end of 2018. Plasma's release will follow in one or more quarters.

Sharding

Vitalik initially proposed the sharding idea for scaling Ethereum blockchain. His proposal was to chop the blockchain into hundreds or thousands of independent pieces: shards. All shards share the same consensus algorithm and security model. These shards will not handle different types of task and do not need to be validated by all full nodes. Instead, each shard serves a single purpose and therefore is very efficient at it. In summary, sharding splits up the state of the network into multiple shards, where each shard has its own transaction history and a portion of the network's state. To implement the sharding idea on the blockchain, a Validator Management Contract is needed, which is a smart contract. It verifies each shard's block headers, maintains validators' stakes, and selects validators between shards pseudo-randomly. Sharding provides an alternative way to increase Ethereum's performance dramatically and could be implemented as early as 2020.

Summary

Ethereum was developed on top of Bitcoin by introducing smart contracts along with Turing-complete scripting languages such as solidity. Ethereum is a general-purpose platform for DApp development. The platform is very popular. However, Ethereum is not mature yet. Compared to Bitcoin, it is more vulnerable to hacking, since any human errors in writing a smart contract are visible to everybody. It inherited the performance issue from Bitcoin. Many initiatives are ongoing to address this scalability problem. In the next chapter, we will dive into the details of solidity, the most popular language for writing Ethereum smart contracts.

3
Overview of Solidity Programming

Solidity is a smart contract programming language. It was developed by Gavin Wood, Christian Reitwiessner, Alex Beregszaszi, and several Ethereum core contributors. It is a JavaScript-like, general-purpose language designed to target the **Ethereum virtual machine** (**EVM**). Solidity is one of four languages in the Ethereum protocol at the same level of abstraction, the others being Serpent (similar to Python), **LLL** (**Lisp-like language**), Vyper (experimental), and Mutan (deprecated). The community has slowly converged on solidity. Usually, if anyone today talks about smart contracts in Ethereum, they implicitly mean solidity.

In this chapter, we will discuss the following topics:

- What is solidity?
- Tools for the solidity development environment
- Introduction to smart contracts
- Common smart contract patterns
- Smart contract security
- Case study – crowdfunding campaign

What is solidity?

Solidity is a statically typed contract language that contains state variables, functions, and common data types. Developers are able to write decentralized applications (DApps) that implement business logic functions in a smart contract. The contract verifies and enforces the constraints at compile time, as opposed to runtime. Solidity is compiled to EVM executable byte code. Once compiled, the contracts are uploaded to the Ethereum network. The blockchain will assign an address to the smart contract. Any permissioned user on the blockchain network can call a contract function to execute the smart contract.

Here is a typical flow diagram showing the process from writing contract code to deploying and running it on the Ethereum network:

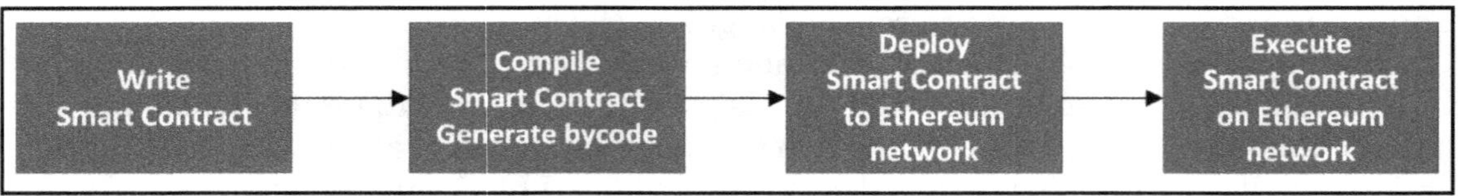

Tools for solidity development environment

Smart contract development is still in its infancy. Creating such contracts and interacting with them in a convenient manner can be done in a multitude of ways. The following powerful tools can be used to build, monitor, and deploy your smart contracts for development on the Ethereum platform.

Browser-based IDE

In this section, we will be looking at onlien browser based tools such as Remix and EthFiddle.

Remix

Remix is a powerful, open source, smart contract tool that helps you write solidity code just from the browser. It supports compile, run, analysis, testing, and debugger options. The following three types of environments are available with Remix when developing and testing:

- **JavaScript VM**: Remix comes with five Ethereum accounts, and each account is deposited with 100 ethers as default. This is convenient for testing smart contracts in the development phase. Mining is not required as it is done automatically. This option is a good choice when you are a beginner.
- **Injected Web3**: This option will directly invoke injected browser web3 instances such as MetaMask, an Ethereum network browser extension. MetaMask provides you with many functions and features, and, like regular Ethereum wallets, it allows you to interact with DApps.
- **Web3 provider**: Remix also supports Web3 provider. The web3.js library is the official Ethereum JavaScript API. It is used to interact with Ethereum smart contracts. You can connect to the blockchain network through web3j API. Web3j supports three different providers: HTTPProvider, WebsocketProvider, and IpcProvider. In Remix Web3, you can give the HTTP URL to connect the remote blockchain instance. The URL can point to your local private blockchain, test-net, and other instance endpoints.

Start by using the Remix solidity IDE: `https://remix.ethereum.org`. The following is the screenshot for the UI of Remix:

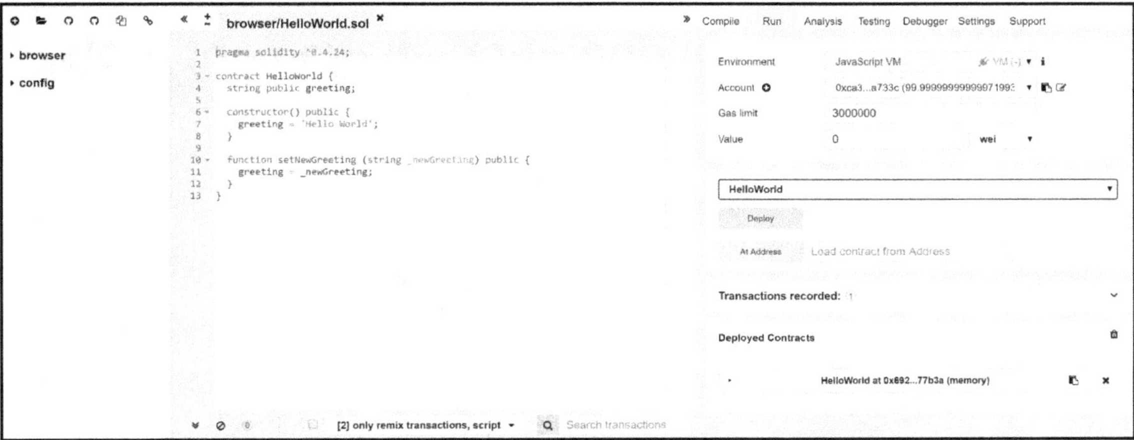

EthFiddle

EthFiddle is a very simple solidity browser-based development tool. You can quickly test and debug smart contract code, and share a permalink to your code. One feature that makes EthFiddle stand out is its potential to perform security audits. The following screenshot shows the software interface:

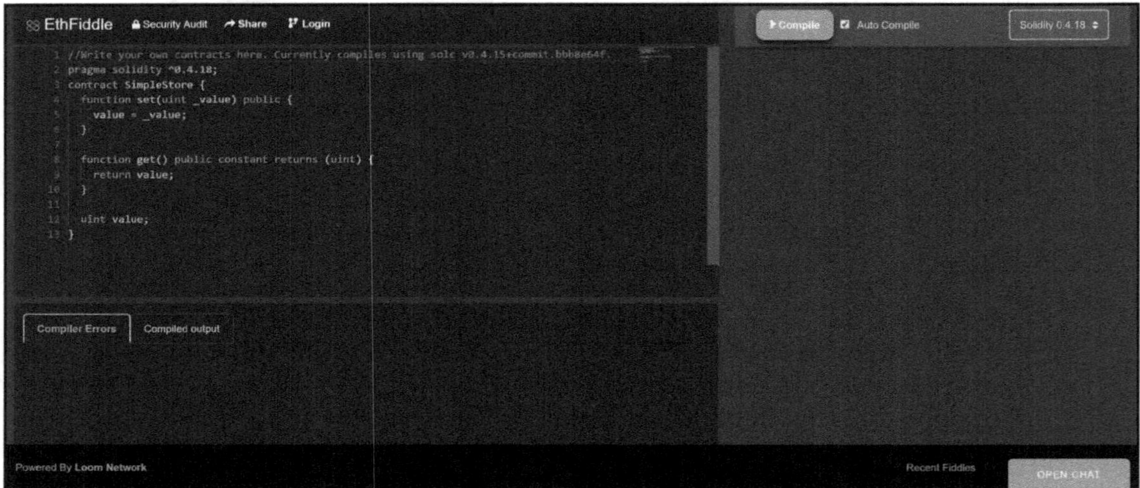

Interface of EthFiddle software

Here is the EthFiddle solidity IDE link: `https://ethfiddle.com`.

Command-line development management tools

The command-line tools are server-side Ethereum tools used to create a basic structure of a DApp project.

Truffle

Truffle is a popular development environment and testing framework, and is an asset pipeline for Ethereum. Truffle's major features include the following:

- Built-in smart contract compilation, linking, deployment, and binary management
- Automated contract testing with Mocha and Chai s Truffle site link: http

- Scriptable deployment and migrations framework
- Network management for deploying to many public and private networks
- Interactive console for direct contract communication
- We will discuss in more detail in the next chapter, and we will use Truffle to development DApp for ERC20 token
- Here is Truffle's site link: `https://truffleframework.com/`

Introduction to smart contracts

Let's begin with the most basic smart contract example, `HelloWorld.sol`, shown as follows:

```
pragma solidity ^0.4.24;

contract HelloWorld {
  string public greeting;

  constructor() public {
    greeting = 'Hello World';
  }

  function setNewGreeting (string _newGreeting) public {
    greeting = _newGreeting;
  }
}
```

Solidity's file extension is `.sol`. It is similar to `.js` for JavaScript files, and `.html` for HTML templates.

Layout of a solidity source file

A solidity source file is typically composed of the following constructs: pragma, comments, and import.

Pragma

The first line containing the keyword pragma simply says that the source code file will not compile with a compiler earlier than version 0.4.24. Anything newer does not break functionality. The ^ symbol implies another condition—the source file will not work either on compilers beyond version 0.5.0.

Comments

Comments are used to make the source code easier for humans to understand the function of the program. Multi-line comments are used for large text descriptions of code. Comments are ignored by the compiler. Multi-line comments start with `/*` and end with `*/`.

In the `HelloWorld` example, there are comments for the `set` and `get` methods:

- Method: The `setNewGreeting (string _newGreeting) {}` function
- `@param`: This is used to indicate what parameters are being passed to a method, and what value they're expected to have

Import

The import keyword in solidity is very similar to JavaScript's past version, ES6. It is used to import libraries and other related features into your solidity source file. Solidity does not support export statements.

Here are a few import examples:

```
import * as symbolName from "solidityFile"
```

The preceding line shown will create a global symbol called `symbolName`, containing the global symbol's member from the import file: `solidityFile`.

Another solidity-specific syntax equivalent to the preceding import is the following:

```
import solidityFile as symbolName;
```

You can also import multiple symbols, and name some of the symbols as alias, demonstrated as follows:

```
import {symbol1 as alias, symbol2} from " solidityFile";
```

Here is an example where an ERC20 token is created using the zeppelin solidity libraries:

```
pragma solidity ^0.4.15;
import 'zeppelin/contracts/math/SafeMath.sol';
....
contract ExampleCoin is ERC20 {
```

```
    //SafeMath symbol is from imported file SafeMath.sol'
    using SafeMath for uint256;
     ...
}
```

For the example shown in the preceding code snippet, we imported the `SafeMath` library from Zeppelin and applied it to `uint256`.

Paths

When importing a solidity file, the file path follows a few simple syntax rules:

- Absolute paths: `/folder1/ folder2/xxx.sol` starting from `/`, the path location is from same solidity file location to the imported files. In our ERC 20 example, this is shown as follows:

```
import 'zeppelin/contracts/math/SafeMath.sol';
```

The actual project structure appears as follows:

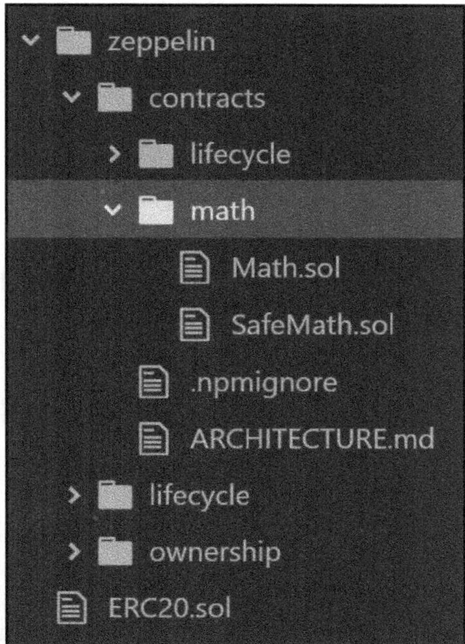

Relative paths

`../folder1/folder2/xxx.sol`: these paths are interpreted relative to the location of the current file, `.` as the current directory, and `..` as the parent directory.

In the solidity path, it is possible to specify path prefix remappings. As an example, if you want to import `github.com/ethereum/dapp-bin/library`, you can first clone the GitHub library to `/usr/local/dapp-bin/library`, and then run the compiler command, shown as follows:

```
solc github.com/ethereum/dapp-bin/library=/usr/local/dapp-bin/library
```

Then, in our solidity file, you can use the following `import` statement. It will remap to `/usr/local/dapp-bin/library/stringUtils.sol`:

```
import "github.com/ethereum/dapp-bin/library/stringUtils.sol " as
stringUtils;
```

The compiler will read the files from there.

Structure of a contract

A contract includes the following constructs: state variables, data type, functions, events, modifiers, enum, struct, and mapping.

State variables

State variables are values that are permanently stored in contract storage, and are used to maintain the contract's state.

The following is an example of the code:

```
contract SimpleStorage {
    uint storedData; // State variable
    //...
}
```

Data type

Solidity is a statically typed language. Developers familiar with language such as JavaScript and Python will find Solidity syntax easy to pick up. Each variable needs to specify the data type. The variable, which will always be passed by value, is called value types, it is built-in or predefined data types.

The value types in solidity are as follows:

<table>
<tr><th>Types</th><th>Operators</th><th>Example</th><th>Note</th></tr>
<tr><td>Bool</td><td>!, &&, ||, ==, !=</td><td>bool a = true;</td><td>The Booleans are true or false expressions.</td></tr>
<tr><td>Int (int8 to int256)</td><td>Comparison operators: <=, <, ==, !=, >=, >,
Bit operators: &, |, ^, +, -, unary -, unary +, *, /, %, **, <<, >></td><td>int a = 1;</td><td>Signed integer, signed of 8 up to 256 bits, in the step of 8.</td></tr>
<tr><td>Uint (uint8 to uint256)</td><td>Comparison operators: <=, <, ==, !=, >=, >
Bit operators: &, |, ^, +, -, unary -, unary +, *, /, %, **, <<, >></td><td>uint maxAge = 100;</td><td>Unsigned integer, unsigned of 8 up to 256 bits, in the step of 8.</td></tr>
<tr><td>Address</td><td><=, <, ==, !=, >= ,></td><td>address owner = msg.sender;
address myAddress = 0xE0f5206B...437b9;</td><td>Holds a 20 byte value (size of an Ethereum address).</td></tr>
<tr><td><address>.balance</td><td></td><td>address.balance()</td><td>Addresses members and <indexentry content="value types, solidity:.balance">returns the balance of the address in Wei.</td></tr>
<tr><td><address>.transfer</td><td></td><td>beneficiary.transfer(highestBid)</td><td>Addresses members and sends ether (in units of Wei) to an address. If the transfer operation fails, it <indexentry content="value types, solidity:.transfer">throws an exception, and all of the changes in a transaction are reverted.</td></tr>
<tr><td><address>.send</td><td></td><td>msg.sender.send(amount)</td><td>Addresses members and send ether (in units of Wei) to an address. If the send operation fails, it returns false.</td></tr>
</table>

<table>
<tr><td><address>.call</td><td></td><td>someAddress.call.
value(1ether)
.gas(100000) ("register", "MyName")</td><td>Executed code of another contract, returns false in the event of failure, forwards all available gas, adjustable, should be used when you need to control how much gas to forward.</td></tr>
<tr><td><address>.delegatecall</td><td></td><td>'
_library.delegatecall(msg.data);</td><td>Executed code of another contract, but with the state (storage) of the calling contract.</td></tr>
<tr><td>Fixed size byte array (bytes1, bytes2, ..., bytes32)</td><td>Comparison operators: <=, <, ==, !=, >=, >,
Bit operators: &, |, ^ ,~,<<, >>,
get array data :
array[index]</td><td>uint8[5] memory traits =
[1,2,3,4,5];</td><td>Fixed size byte arrays are defined using the keyword byteN, the N being any number from 1 to 32, it limits the size, it will be a lot cheaper and will save you gas.</td></tr>
<tr><td>Dynamically-sized array bytes string</td><td></td><td>/**bytes array **/
bytes32[] dynamicArray
function f() {
        bytes32[] storage
storageArr = dynamicArray
        storageArr.length++;
}
/**string array **/
bytes32[] public names</td><td>Solidity supports a dynamically-sized byte array and a dynamically-sized UTF-8-encoded string.</td></tr>
<tr><td>Hexadecimal literals</td><td></td><td>hex"1AF34A"</td><td>Hexadecimal literals are prefixed with the keyword hex and are enclosed in single or double quotes.</td></tr>
<tr><td>Address literals</td><td></td><td>0x5eD8Cee6b63b1c6AFce
3AD7c92f4fD7E1B8fAd9F</td><td>It is hexadecimal literals that pass the address checksum test.</td></tr>
<tr><td>String literals</td><td></td><td>"Hello"</td><td>String literals are normally written with either single or double quotes.</td></tr>
</table>

Enum type

Enum is a type with a restricted set of constants values. Here is an example, as follows:

```
pragma solidity ^0.4.24;
  contract ColorEnum {
    enum Color {RED,ORANGE,YELLOW, GREEN}
    Color color;
    function construct() public {
     color = Color.RED;
    }
    function setColor(uint _value) public {
      color = Color(_value);
    }
  function getColor() public view returns (uint){
      return uint(color);
  }
}
```

Struct type

A struct is a type that contains named fields. New types can be declared using struct. Here is an example in the following code:

```
struct person {
         uint age;
         string fName;
         string lName;
         string email;
    }
```

Mapping

Mappings act as hash tables that consist of key types and corresponding value type pairs. Here is an example, as follows:

```
pragma solidity ^0.4.24;
contract StudentScore {
    struct Student {
        uint score;
        string name;
    }
    mapping (address => Student) studtents;
    address[] public studentAccts;
    function setStudent(address _address, uint _score, string _name) public
```

```
{
        Student storage studtent = studtents[_address];
        studtent.score = _score;
        studtent.name = _name;
        studentAccts.push(_address) -1;
    }
    function getStudents() view public returns(address[]) {
        return studentAccts;
    }
    function getStudent(address _address) view public returns (uint,
string) {
        return (studtents[_address].score, studtents[_address].name);
    }
    function countStudents() view public returns (uint) {
        return studentAccts.length;
    }
}
```

Functions

Functions are the executable units of code within a contract. Here is a function structure in solidity, as follows:

```
function (<Input parameters>) {access modifiers}
[pure|constant|view|payable] [returns (<return types>)]
```

Input parameters

Function can pass input parameters. The input parameters are declared the same way as variables are.

In the previous `HelloWorld` example, we define `setNewGreeting` using the input parameter, `string _newGreeting`. Here is an example of this step:

```
function setNewGreeting (string _newGreeting) {
  greeting = _newGreeting;
}
```

Access modifiers

Solidity access modifiers are used to provide access control in Solidity.

There are four types of access modifiers available in Solidity, listed as follows:

- **Public**: Accessible from this contract, inherited contracts, and externally
- **Private**: Accessible only from this contract
- **Internal**: Accessible only from this contract and contracts inheriting from it
- **External**: Cannot be accessed internally, only externally

Output parameters

The output parameters can be declared after the `return` keyword, as shown in the following code snippet:

```
function getColor() public view returns (uint){
     return uint(color);
  }
```

In solidity, `pure` functions are functions that are promised not to modify, or read the state.

```
pure|constant|view|payable
```

If the function modifier is defined as view, it indicates that the function will not change the storage state.

If the function modifier is defined as pure, it indicates that the function will not read the storage state.

If the function modifier is defined as constant, it indicates that the function won't modify the contract storage.

If the function modifier is defined as payable, modifier can receive funds.

```
uint amount =0;
function buy() public payable{
    amount += msg.value;
}
```

In the preceding example, the `buy` function has a payable modifier, which makes sure you can send ethers to the `buy` function. A function without any name, and annotated with a payable keyword, is called a payable fallback function.

```
pragma solidity ^0.4.24;
// this is a contract, which keeps all Ether to it with not way of
// retrieving it.
contract MyContract {
    function() public payable { }
}
```

Modifiers

In solidity, the modifier is used to change the behavior of a function. They can automatically check a condition prior to executing the function. Here is an example, as follows:

```
pragma solidity ^0.4.24;
contract Modifiers {
         address public admin;
    function construct () public {
       admin = msg.sender;
    }
    //define the modifiers
    modifier onlyAdmin() {
        // if a condition is not met then throw an exception
        if (msg.sender != admin) revert();
        // or else just continue executing the function
        _;
    }
    // apply modifiers

    function kill() onlyAdmin public {
         selfdestruct(admin);
    }
}
```

Events

Events are used to track the execution of a transaction sent to a contract. There are convenient interfaces with the EVM logging facilities. Here is an example, as follows:

```
pragma solidity ^0.4.24;
contract Purchase {
    event buyEvent(address bidder, uint amount); // Event
    function buy() public payable {
        emit buyEvent(msg.sender, msg.value); // Triggering event
    }
}
```

Constructor

The constructor method is a special method for creating and initializing a contract. In solidity v0.4.23, Solidity introduced this new constructor notation and the old one was deprecated.

```
//new
pragma solidity ^0.4.24;
contract HelloWorld {
  function constructor() public {
    // ...
  }
}
//deprecated
pragma solidity ^0.4.22;
contract HelloWorld {
  function HelloWorld () public {
    // ...
  }
}
```

Constant state variables, unit, and functions

The value of a constant cannot change through reassignment, and it can't be redeclared after compile time. In solidity, a state variable can be declared as constant. It does not allow reassignment to blockchain data (for example, this `.balance`, `block.blockhash`), or execution data (`tx.gasprice`), or make calls to external contracts.

The following table out the solidity global variables and their built-in functions:

Global variables / functions	Description
`msg.sender(address)`	`msg.sender` is the address currently interacting with the contract call message.
`msg.data(bytes)`	`msg.data` is the address currently interacting with the contract complete call. The data is in bytes.
`msg.value(unit)`	`msg.value` is the address currently interacting with the number of Wei sent with message as per the contract.
`msg.sig`	`msg.sig` is the address currently interacting with the contract that returns the first four bytes of the call data.
`gasleft() returns (uint256)`	API to check the gas remaining.
`tx.origin`	API to check the sender of the transaction.
`tx.gasprice`	API to check the gas price of the transaction.
`now`	Get current unix timestamp.
`block.number`	API to retrieve the current block number.
`block.difficulty`	API to retrieve the current block difficulty.
`block.blockhash(uint blockNumber) returns (bytes32)`	API to get the hash of the given block; the result only returned the 256 most recent blocks.
`block.gasLimit(unit)`	API to get the current block gas limit.
`block.coinbase ()`	Returns the current block miner's address.
`keccak256(...);`	Returns (bytes32) compute the Ethereum-SHA-3 (Keccak-256) hash of the (tightly packed) arguments.
`sha3(...)`	Returns (bytes32): an alias to keccak256.
`assert(bool condition)`	`assert` can be used to check for conditions. It indicates something that should never be false under any circumstances. Furthermore, `assert` uses the `0xfe` opcode to cause an error condition.
`require(bool condition)`	The `require` function should be used to ensure valid conditions. It can return false when the user enters something inappropriate. Furthermore, `require()` uses the `0xfd` opcode to cause an error condition.
`revert()`	`revert` will still undo all state changes.
`<address>.balance`	It checks the balance of the address in Wei (uint256).
`<address>.send(uint256 amount) returns (bool)`	API sends the amount of Wei to address and returns false in the event failure.
`<address>.transfer(uint256 amount)`	API transfer the amount of Wei to the address, and throws error when transfer fails.
`this`	The current contract, explicitly convertible to address.
`super`	The contract one level higher in the inheritance hierarchy.
`selfdestruct(address recipient)`	`self-destruct` will destroy the current contract, and storage associated with it is removed from the Ethereum's world state.
`suicide(address recipient)`	An alias to self-destruct.

Ether units

Solidity ether is dividable into Wei, Kwei, Mwei, Gwei, Szabo, Finney, Kether, Mether, Gether, and Tether. The following are the conversion units:

- 1 ether = 1,000 Finney
- 1 Finney = 1,000 Szabo
- 1 Szabo = 1,000 Mwei

- 1 Mwei = 1,000 Kwei
- 1 Kwei = 1,000 Wei

Time units

A solidity time unit is dividable into seconds, minutes, hours, days, weeks, and years. The following are the conversion units:

- 1 = 1 second
- 1 minute = 60 seconds
- 1 hour = 60 minutes
- 1 day = 24 hours
- 1 week = 7 days
- 1 year = 365 days

Inheritance, abstract, and interface

Many of the most widely used programming languages (such as C++, Java, Go, and Python, and so on) support **object-oriented programming** (**OOP**) and support inheritance, encapsulation, abstraction, and polymorphism. Inheritance enables code reuse and extensibility. Solidity supports multiple inheritance in the form of copying code, which includes polymorphism. Even if a contract inherits from multiple other contracts, only a single contract is created on the blockchain.

In solidity, inheritance is pretty similar to classic oriented-object programming languages. Here are a number of examples, as follows:

```
pragma solidity ^0.4.24;
contract Animal {
    constructor() public {
    }
    function name() public returns (string) {
        return  "Animal";
    }
    function color() public returns (string);
}
contract Mammal is Animal {
    int size;
    constructor() public {
    }
    function name() public returns (string) {
        return  "Mammal";
```

```
        }
        function run() public pure returns (int) {
            return 10;
        }
        function color() public returns (string);
    }
    contract Dog is Mammal {
         function name() public returns (string) {
            return  "Dog";
        }
        function color() public returns (string) {
            return "black";
        }
    }
```

Dog inherits from `Mammal`, whose parent contract is `Animal`. When calling `Dog.run()`, it will call its parent method `run()` and return ten. When calling name, `Dog.name()` will override its patent method and return the output from `Dog`.

In solidity, a method without a body (no implementation) is known as an abstract method. A contract that contains an abstract method cannot be instantiated, but can be used as a base.

If a contract inherits from an abstract contract, then the contract must implement all the abstract methods of abstract parent class, or it has to be declared abstract as well.

Dog has a concrete `color()` method, which is a concrete contract and can be compiled, but the parent contract—mammal, and the grandparent contract—animal, are still abstract contracts.

Interfaces in solidity are similar to abstract contracts; they are implicitly abstract and cannot have implementations. An abstract contract can have instance methods that implement a default behavior. There are more restrictions in interfaces, as follows:

- Cannot inherit other contracts or interfaces
- Cannot define constructor
- Cannot define variables
- Cannot define structs
- Cannot define enums

```
pragma solidity ^0.4.24;
//interface
contract A {
    function doSomething() public returns (string);
}
```

```
//contract implements interface A
contract B is A {
    function doSomething() public returns (string) {
        return "Hello";
    }
}
```

In the preceding example, the contract is an interface, `contract B` implements `interface A`, and has a concrete `doSomething()` method.

Common smart contract patterns

In this section, we will discuss some common design and programming patterns for the smart contract programming language.

Access restriction

Access restriction is a solidity security pattern. It only allows authorized parties to access certain functions. Due to the public nature of the blockchain, all data on the blockchain is visible to anyone. It is critical to declare your contract function, state with restricted access control, and provide security against unauthorized access to smart contract functionality.

```
pragma solidity ^0.4.24;
contract Ownable {
 address owner;
 uint public initTime = now;
 constructor() public {
 owner = msg.sender;
 }
 //check if the caller is the owner of the contract
 modifier onlyOwner {
 require(msg.sender == owner,"Only Owner Allowed." );
 _;
 }
 //change the owner of the contract
 //@param _newOwner the address of the new owner of the contract.
 function changeOwner(address _newOwner) public onlyOwner {
 owner = _newOwner;
 }
 function getOwner() internal constant returns (address) {
 return owner;
 }
 modifier onlyAfter(uint _time) {
```

```
    require(now >= _time,"Function called too early.");
    _;
    }
    modifier costs(uint _amount) {
    require(msg.value >= _amount,"Not enough Ether provided." );
    _;
    if (msg.value > _amount)
    msg.sender.transfer(msg.value - _amount);
    }
   }
   contract SampleContarct is Ownable {


    mapping(bytes32 => uint) myStorage;
    constructor() public {
    }
    function getValue(bytes32 record) constant public returns (uint) {
    return myStorage[record];
    }
    function setValue(bytes32 record, uint value) public onlyOwner {
    myStorage[record] = value;
    }
    function forceOwnerChange(address _newOwner) public payable
   onlyOwner onlyAfter(initTime + 2 weeks) costs(50 ether) {
    owner =_newOwner;
    initTime = now;
    }
   }
```

The preceding example shows the access restrict pattern applied to a contract. We first define a parent class called `Ownable` with `onlyOwner`, `changeOwner`, and `onlyAfter` function modifiers. Other contracts can inherit from this contract to use defined access restriction. `SampleContract` inherits from `Ownable` contract and therefore, only the owner can access `setValue` function. Furthermore, `forceOwnerChange` may only be called two weeks after the contract creation time with 50 ether cost, and only the owner has permission to execute the function.

State machine

State machine is a behavior design pattern. It allows a contract to alter its behavior when it's internal state changes. A smart contract function call typically moves a contract state from one stage to the next stage. The basic operation of a state machine has two parts:

- It traverses through a sequence of states, where the next state is determined by the present state, and input conditions.
- It provides sequences of outputs based upon state transitions.

To illustrate this, let's develop a simple state machine. We will use washing dishes as an example. The process typically is *scrub, rinse, dry, scrub, rinse, dry*. We defined state machine stages as an enumerated type. As this is an extensive use case, only the state machine related code is presented. Any logic for detailed action implementation, such as `rinse()`, `dry()` and so on are omitted. See the following example:

```
pragma solidity ^0.4.24;
contract StateMachine {
 enum Stages {
 INIT,
 SCRUB,
 RINSE,
 DRY,
 CLEANUP
 }


 Stages public stage = Stages.INIT;
 modifier atStage(Stages _stage) {
 require(stage == _stage);
 _;
 }
 function nextStage() internal {
 stage = Stages(uint(stage) + 1);
 }
 modifier transitionNext() {
 _;
 nextStage();
 }

 function scrub() public atStage(Stages.INIT) transitionNext {
 // Implement scrub logic here
 }


 function rinse() public atStage(Stages.SCRUB) transitionNext {
```

```
    // Implement rinse logic here
    }

    function dry() public atStage(Stages.SCRUB) transitionNext {
    // Implement dry logic here
    }

    function cleanup() public view atStage(Stages.CLEANUP) {
    // Implement dishes cleanup
    }
  }
```

We define function modifier `atStage` to check if the current state allows the stage to run the function. Furthermore, `transitionNext` modifier will call the internal method `nextStage()` to move state to next stage.

Smart contract security

Once a smart contract has been deployed on the Ethereum network, it is immutable and public to everyone. Many of the smart contract functions are account payment related; therefore, security and testing become absolutely essential for a contract before being deployed on the main network. Following are security practices that will help you better design and write flawless Ethereum smart contracts.

Keep contract simple and modular

Try to keep your smart contract small, simple, and modularized. Complicated code is difficult to read, understand, and debug, it is also error-prone.

Use well-written library tools where possible.

Limit the amount of local variables.

Move unrelated functionality to other contracts or libraries.

Use the checks-effects-interactions pattern

Be very careful when interacting with other external contracts, it should be the last step in your function. It can introduce several unexpected risks or errors. External calls may execute malicious code. These kinds of calls should be considered as potential security risks and avoided if possible.

```
pragma solidity ^0.4.24;
// THIS CONTRACT is INSECURE - DO NOT USE
contract Fund {
    mapping(address => uint) userBalances;
function withdrawBalance() public {
     //external call
         if (msg.sender.call.value(userBalances[msg.sender])())
            userBalances[msg.sender] = 0;
}
}
contract Hacker {
    Fund f;
    uint public count;
    event LogWithdrawFallback(uint c, uint balance);
    function Attacker(address vulnerable) public {
        f = Fund(vulnerable);
    }
    function attack() public {
        f.withdrawBalance();
    }


    function () public payable {
        count++;
        emit LogWithdrawFallback(count, address(f).balance);
        if (count < 10) {
          f.withdrawBalance();
        }
    }
  }
}
```

The line `msg.sender.call.value(userBalances[msg.sender])` is an external call, when `withdrawBalance` is called, it will send ether with the `address.call.value()`. The hacker can attack fund contracts by triggering the hack fallback function, which can call the `withdrawBalance` method again. This will allow the attacker to refund multiple times, draining all ether in accounts.

The preceding contract vulnerabilities is called reentrancy. To avoid this, you can use the checks-effects-interactions pattern, shown in the following example:

```
pragma solidity ^0.4.24;
contract Fund {
    mapping(address => uint) userBalances;
    funct
ion withdrawBalance() public {
        uint amt = userBalances[msg.sender];
        userBalances[msg.sender] =0;
        msg.sender.transfer(amt);
    }
}
```

We first need to identify which part of the function involves external calls, `uint amt = userBalances[msg.sender]; userBalances[msg.sender] =0;`.

The function reads `userBalances` value, and assigns it to a local variable, then it resets `userBalances`. These steps are to make sure message sender can only transfer to their own account, but can't make any changes to state variables. The balance of a user will be reduced before the ether is actually transferred to user. If any error occurs during the transfer, the whole transaction will be reverted, including the reduction transfer amount of balance in the state variable. This approach can be described as *optimistic accounting*, because effects are written down as completed, before they actually take place.

DoS with block gas limit

The Ethereum blockchain transaction can only process a certain amount of gas due to the block gas limit, so be careful to look without fixed limited integration. When a number of iteration costs go beyond the gas limit, the transaction will fail and the contract can be stalled at a certain point. In this case, attackers may potentially attack the contract, and manipulate the gas.

Handle errors in external calls

As we discussed earlier, solidity has some low-level call methods: `address.call()`, `address.callcode()`, `address.delegatecall()`, and `address.send()`. These methods only return false when the call encounters an exception. So handling errors in external calls is very important in contracts, as shown in the following code snippet:

```
// good
if(!contractAddress.send(100)) {
```

```
    // handle error
}
contractAddress.send(20);//don't do this
contractAddress.call.value(55)(); // this is doubly dangerous, as it will
forward all remaining gas and doesn't check for result
contractAddress.call.value(50)(bytes4(sha3("withdraw()"))); // if withdraw
throws an exception, the raw call() will only return false and transaction
will NOT be reverted
```

Case study – crowdfunding campaign

In this section, we will implement and deploy the smart contract for the crowdfunding campaign use case.

The idea of crowd funding is a process of raising funds for a project or venture from the masses. Investors receive tokens that represent a share of the startup they invested. The project sets up a predefined goal and a deadline for reaching it. Once a project misses the goal, the investments are returned, which reduces the risk for investors. This decentralized fundraising model can supplant the fund need for startup, and there is no need for a centralized trusted platform. Investors will only pay the gas fees if the fund returns. Any project contributor gets a token, and they can trade, sell, or keep these tokens. In a certain stage, the token can be used in exchange for real products as the physical reward.

Define struct and events, shown as follows:

```
pragma solidity ^0.4.24;

contract CrowdFunding {

    Project public project;
    Contribution[] public contributions;
    //Campaign Status
    enum Status {
        Fundraising,
        Fail,
        Successful
    }
    event LogProjectInitialized (
        address owner,
        string name,
        string website,
        uint minimumToRaise,
        uint duration
    );
    event ProjectSubmitted(address addr, string name, string url, bool
```

```
initialized);
    event LogFundingReceived(address addr, uint amount, uint currentTotal);
    event LogProjectPaid(address projectAddr, uint amount, Status status);
    event Refund(address _to, uint amount);
    event LogErr (address addr, uint amount);
    //campaign contributors
    struct Contribution {
        address addr;
        uint amount;
    }
    //define project
    struct Project {
        address addr;
        string name;
        string website;
        uint totalRaised;
        uint minimumToRaise;
        uint currentBalance;
        uint deadline;
        uint completeAt;
        Status status;
    }
    //initialized project
    constructor (address _owner, uint _minimumToRaise, uint
_durationProjects,
        string _name, string _website) public payable {
        uint minimumToRaise = _minimumToRaise * 1 ether; //convert to wei
        uint deadlineProjects = now + _durationProjects* 1 seconds;
        project = Project(_owner, _name, _website, 0, minimumToRaise, 0,
deadlineProjects, 0, Status.Fundraising);
        emit LogProjectInitialized(
            _owner,
            _name,
            _website,
            _minimumToRaise,
            _durationProjects);
    }
```

Define modifiers, shown in the following code:

```
    //check if project is at the required stage
     modifier atStage(Status _status) {
         require(project.status == _status,"Only matched status allowed." );
         _;
     }
     //check if msg.sender is project owner
     modifier onlyOwner() {
         require(project.addr == msg.sender,"Only Owner Allowed." );
         _;
     }
     //check if project pass the deadline
     modifier afterDeadline() {
         require(now >= project.deadline);
         _;
     }
     //Wait for 6 hour after campaign completed before allowing contract
destruction
     modifier atEndOfCampain() {
         require(!((project.status == Status.Fail || project.status ==
Status.Successful) && project.completeAt + 6 hours < now));
         _;
     }
```

Define smart contract functions, shown as follows:

```
    function () public payable {
        revert();
     }

     /* The default fallback function is called whenever anyone sends funds
to a contract */
     function fund() public atStage(Status.Fundraising) payable {
         contributions.push(
             Contribution({
                 addr: msg.sender,
                 amount: msg.value
                 })
             );
         project.totalRaised += msg.value;
         project.currentBalance = project.totalRaised;
         emit LogFundingReceived(msg.sender, msg.value,
project.totalRaised);
     }
     //checks if the goal or time limit has been reached and ends the
campaign
     function checkGoalReached() public onlyOwner afterDeadline {
```

```
        require(project.status != Status.Successful &&
project.status!=Status.Fail);
        if (project.totalRaised > project.minimumToRaise){
            project.addr.transfer(project.totalRaised);
            project.status = Status.Successful;
            emit LogProjectPaid(project.addr, project.totalRaised,
project.status);
        } else {
            project.status = Status.Fail;
            for (uint i = 0; i < contributions.length; ++i) {
              uint amountToRefund = contributions[i].amount;
              contributions[i].amount = 0;
              if(!contributions[i].addr.send(contributions[i].amount)) {
                contributions[i].amount = amountToRefund;
                emit LogErr(contributions[i].addr,
contributions[i].amount);
                revert();
              } else{
                project.totalRaised -= amountToRefund;
                project.currentBalance = project.totalRaised;
                emit Refund(contributions[i].addr,
contributions[i].amount);
              }
            }
        }
        project.completeAt = now;
    }
    function destroy() public onlyOwner atEndOfCampain {
        selfdestruct(msg.sender);
    }
}
```

Let's use Remix to test our campaign. We select the JavaScript VM option.

1. Initialize the campaign by clicking the **Deploy** button with the following input. This will start our campaign by means of the call constructor. We assign the first account as the project owner. The minimum funds raised is 30 ether, deadline set to five minutes for testing purposes. Put the following input code in the text box beside the **Deploy** button. Here are input parameters for constructor:

```
0xca35b7d915458ef540ade6068dfe2f44e8fa733c, 30, 100, "smartchart",
"smartchart.tech"
```

The following is the screenshot for the Remix editor screen for this step:

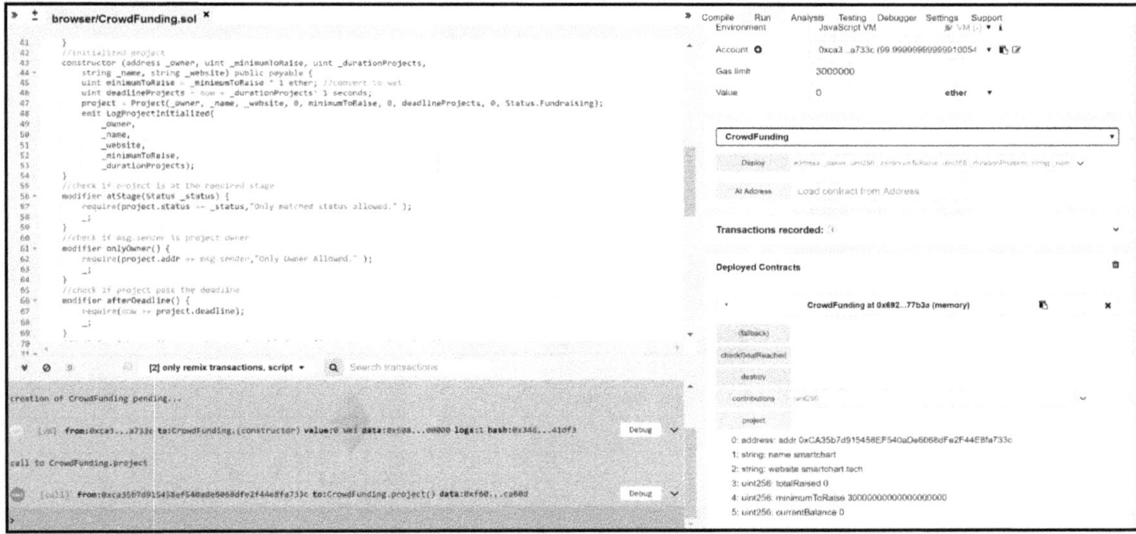

Remix editor screen

2. Switch to the second account and, in the Remix value input field, enter `20` ether, and then click **(fallback)** button. This will add `20` ether to **totalRaised**. To check project information, click project button, and you should see that the **totalRaised** is 20 ethers now. Enter `0` uint in the **contributions** input field, and we can a see second account contribution address, and a fund amount of 20 ethers:

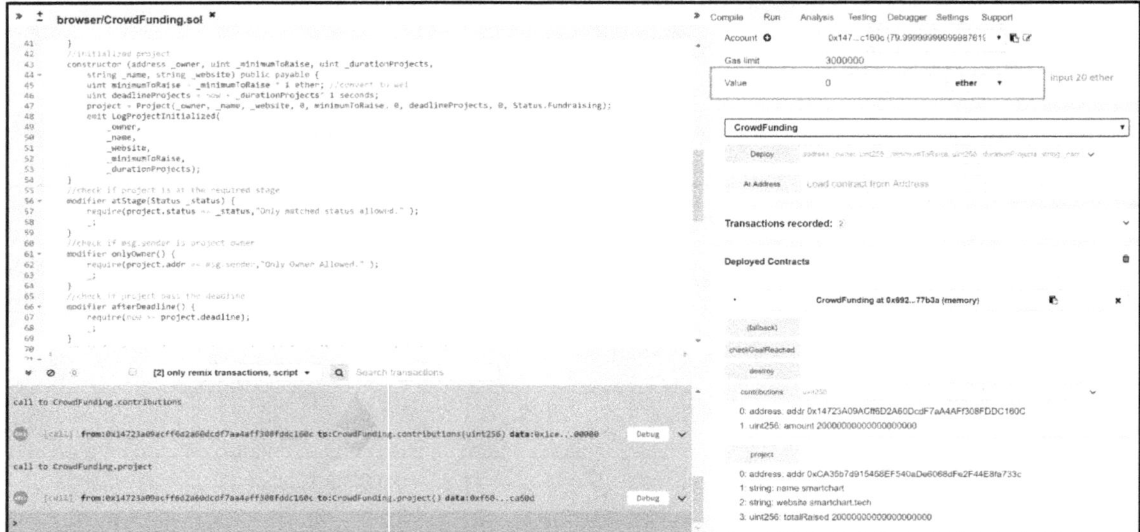

Remix value input field

3. Switch to the third account, enter `15` ethers in the **Value** field to add funds for the project. Click **(fallback)**, and we can see the project total fund raised to **35** ethers. At this moment, the project has achieved the campaign goal:

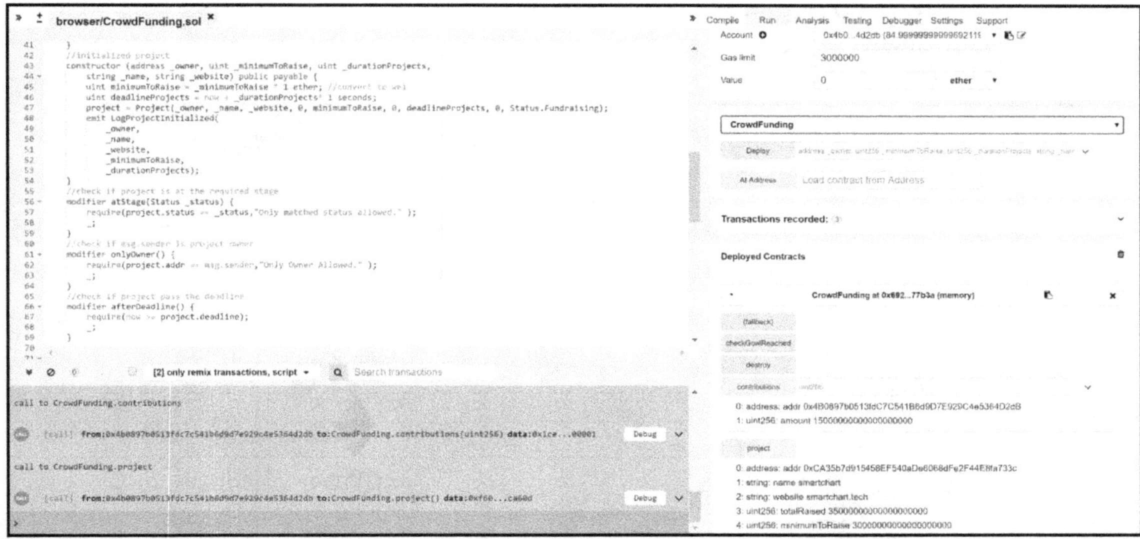

Adding funds to the project

4. Switch back to project owner, which is the first account, and click **checkGoalReached.** We can see that the transaction has been successfully executed. In the logs, the project status is updated to "successful". `LogProjectPaid` is triggered. If we check Remix account 1, 2, 3, the project owner account now contains a total in the region of 135 ethers. Our campaign smart contract was successfully tested in Remix:

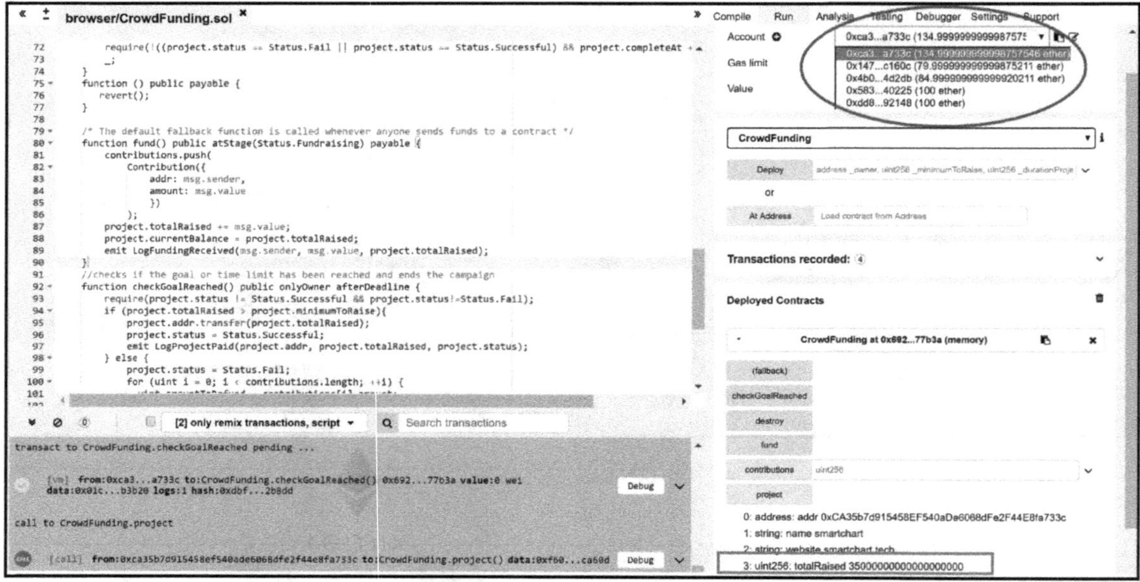

Successfully testing the campaign in smart contract

Summary

In this chapter, we learned the basic features of solidity programming. We also overviewed current popular smart contract development tools. By exploring common patterns and security best practices, we learned how to write better code to avoid contract vulnerabilities. Finally, we wrote a crowd funding campaign contract, and used Remix to deploy and test our example.

In the next chapter, we will build a Decentralize application (DApp) for crowdfunding.

4
Building an Ethereum Blockchain Application

In the previous chapter, we reviewed the basic features of smart contracts and how to write a crowdfunding smart contract example. After we deployed the smart contract to the blockchain, we needed to write the web application to interact with the smart contract. Ethereum blockchain provides the web3 API by calling smart contract functions and getters.

In this chapter, we will cover the following topics:

- What is a **decentralized application** (**DApp**)
- web3js quick overview
- Setting up an Ethereum development environment
- Developing and testing a DApp

Decentralized application overview

A **decentralized application** (or **DApp**) is an application that uses smart contracts to run. Smart contracts are deployed on the **Ethereum virtual machine** (**EVM**). It is similar to a client-server low-tier architecture. A DApp can have a frontend (web) that makes calls to its backend (smart contract) through the web3.js API.

The following structure is what we are going to build for our crowdfunding DApp:

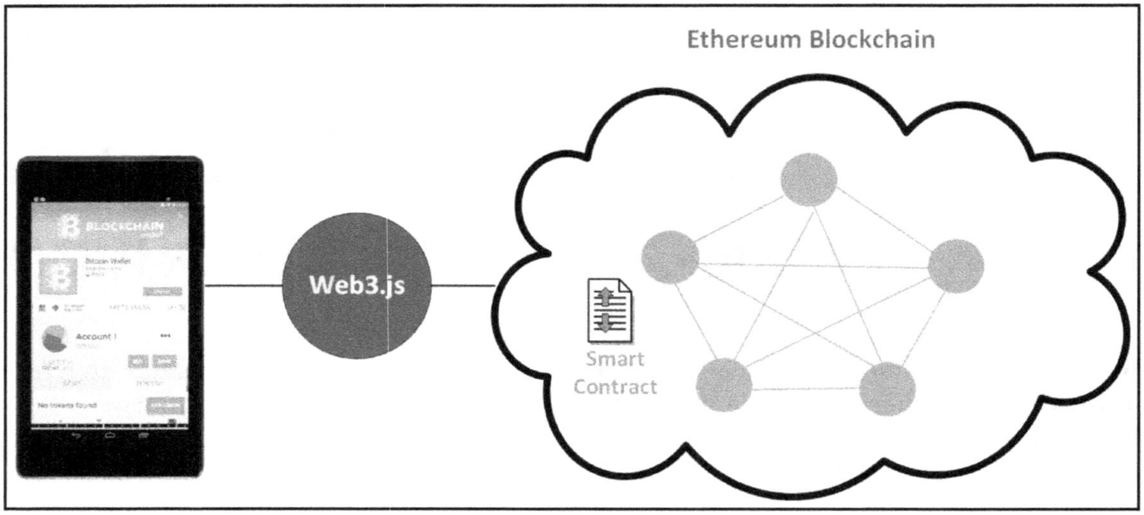

Strucuture of what we will be building for crowdfunding DApp

web3.js quick overview

web3.js is an Ethereum JavaScript API, that provides a collection of libraries to interact with a local or remote Ethereum network. The connection between web3js and Ethereum is made by using the HTTP or IPC protocol. In the following table, we quickly review a number of important web3.js API concepts:

API reference	Description	Example
web3-eth	This package provides an API to interact with the Ethereum blockchain and smart contracts	`getBalance`, `sendTransaction`, `coinbase`, `getBlockNumber`, `getAccounts`
web3-shh	This package provides an API to interact with the whisper protocol for broadcasting	`web3.shh.post({ symKeyID: identities[0], topic: '0xffaadd11', payload: '0xffffffdddddd1122' }).then(h => console.log(`Message with hash ${h} was successfuly sent`))`

web3-bzz	This package provides an API to interact with the Ethereum swarm, the decentralized file storage platform	`web3.bzz.currentProvider` `web3.bzz.download(bzzHash [, localpath])`
web3-utils	This package provides a collection of utility functions for Ethereum DApps and other web3.js packages	`web3.utils.toWei(number [, unit])` `web3.utils.isAddress(address)`

Provider

A provider abstracts a connection that talks to the Ethereum blockchain. It will issue queries and send transactions to the blockchain. web3 provides `JsonRpcProvider` and `IpcProvider`, which allow you to connect to a local or remote Ethereum node, including Mainnet, Ropsten testnet, Kovan testnet, Rinkeby testnet, and custom **remote procedure call** (**RPC**), like Ganache. Below is the code snippet to show how we can use web3 API to connect an Ethereum node.

```
var Web3 = require('web3');
var web3 = new Web3('http://localhost:8545');
// or
var web3 = new Web3(new
Web3.providers.HttpProvider('http://localhost:8545'));
// change provider
web3.setProvider('ws://localhost:8546');
// or
web3.setProvider(new
Web3.providers.WebsocketProvider('ws://localhost:8546'));
```

DApp development tools

There are some popular blockchain web development tools used being by developers for creating a basic structure of a DApp project. The following sections list a few of these.

Truffle

Truffle is an Ethereum DApp end-to-end development tool that provides a development environment for writing, compiling, and deploying test smart contracts and DApps. You can write HTML, CSS, and JavaScript for the frontend; Solidity is for smart contracts, and uses the web3.js API to interact with the UI and smart contract. Truffle Boxes provide helpful boilerplates, which contain helpful modules, solidity contracts and libraries, frontend code, and many other helpful files. The Truffle Boxes help developers to quickly get started with their DApp project.

The Truffle command line uses the following formats:

- `truffle [command] [options]`

Here are the frequently used options in command-line tools:

command	**Description**
`compile`	Compile solidity contract files.
`console`	Command-line interface to interact with deployed smart contracts.
`create`	This command helps to create a new contract, new migration file, and basic test.
`debug`	Experiment on a particular transaction in debugger sessions.
`deploy/migration`	Deploy a contract to the blockchain network.
`develop`	Interact with a contract via the command line in the local development environment.
`init`	Install a package from the Ethereum package registry.

Ganache

Ganache is a private Ethereum blockchain environment that allows to you emulate the Ethereum blockchain so that you can interact with smart contracts in your own private blockchain. Here are some features that Ganache provides:

- Displays blockchain log output
- Provides advanced mining control
- Built-in block explorer
- Ethereum blockchain environment
- Ganache has a desktop application as well as a command-line tool

This is what the desktop version of Ganache looks like:

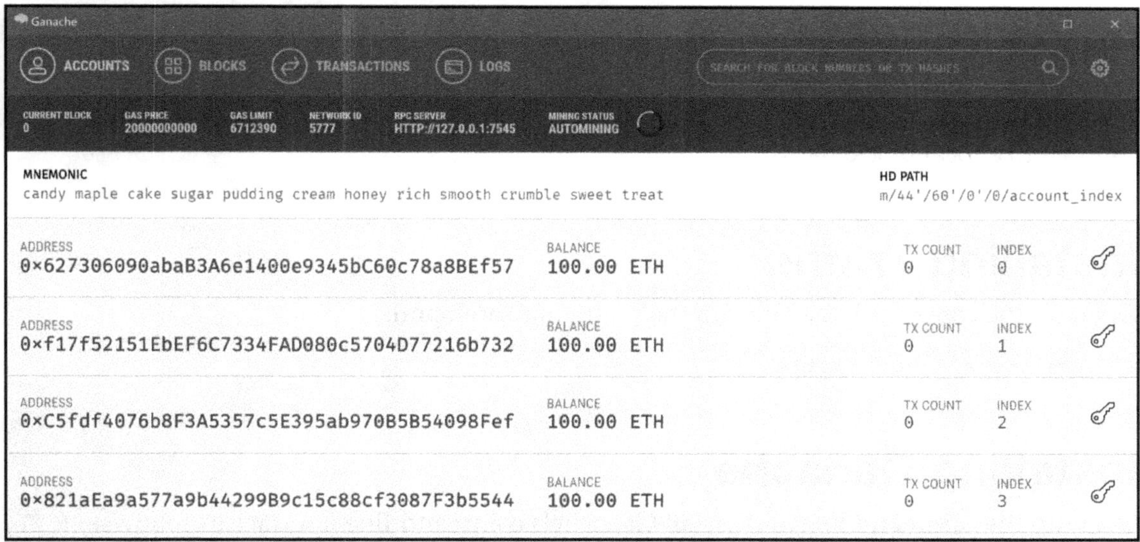

The command line uses the following format:

```
ganache-cli <options>
```

These are the frequently used options of the command-line tools:

Options	Description
`-a or --accounts`	The number of accounts to generate at startup.
`-e or --defaultBalanceEther`	Configure the default test account ether amount. The default is `100`.
`-b or --blockTime`	Specify the block time in seconds as a mining interval. If this option is not specified, Ganache will instantly mine a new block when a transaction is invoked.
`-h or --host or --hostname`	Specify hostname to listen on. The default is `127.0.0.1`.
`-p or --port`	Specify the port number. The default is `8545`.
`-g or --gasPrice`	Specify the gas price in Wei (defaults to `20000000000`).
`-l or --gasLimit`	The block gas limit (defaults to `0x6691b7`).
`--debug`	Display VM opcodes for debugging purpose.
`-q or --quiet`	Run `ganache-cli` without any logs.

Setting up an Ethereum development environment

Follow these instructions to obtain the Ethereum development tools and start up an Ethereum private local blockchain environment (primarily used to run/deploy your smart contract to a local blockchain).

Installing Truffle

Open up the command line and run the following command:

```
npm install -g truffle
```

Installing Ganache

Open up the command line and install Ganache's command-line interface as follows:

```
npm install -g ganache-cli
```

Creating a Truffle project

To initialize a new DApp project, we can run the truffle `init` command to initialize an empty Truffle project. This will create the DApp directory structure, including apps, contracts, and tests with Truffle configurations. Since Truffle Boxes provide many working templates, in our DApp example, we will use pet-shop box—a JQuery version of a JavaScript UI library—to develop our crowdfunding DApp example.

Create a folder called `Crowdfunding`, open a command-line prompt, navigate to the `Crowdfunding` folder, and run the following command:

```
truffle unbox pet-shop
```

The project structure is as follows:

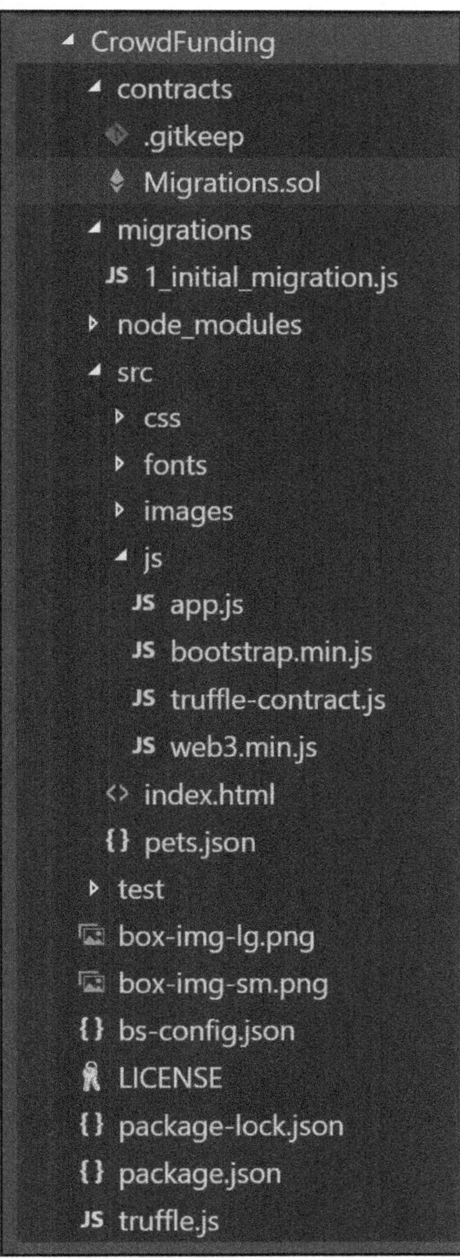

We wrote the crowdfunding smart contract in the previous chapter. Let's copy the `CrowdFunding.sol` file into the contracts folder under `Crowdfunding`.

Launching the Ganache environment

Open a new Terminal window and run the following command:

```
Ganache-cli
```

This will run `Ganache-cli` on port `8545`, and Ganache will create 10 default accounts for us. Each account will have 100 ether by default. You should see something like this in your console:

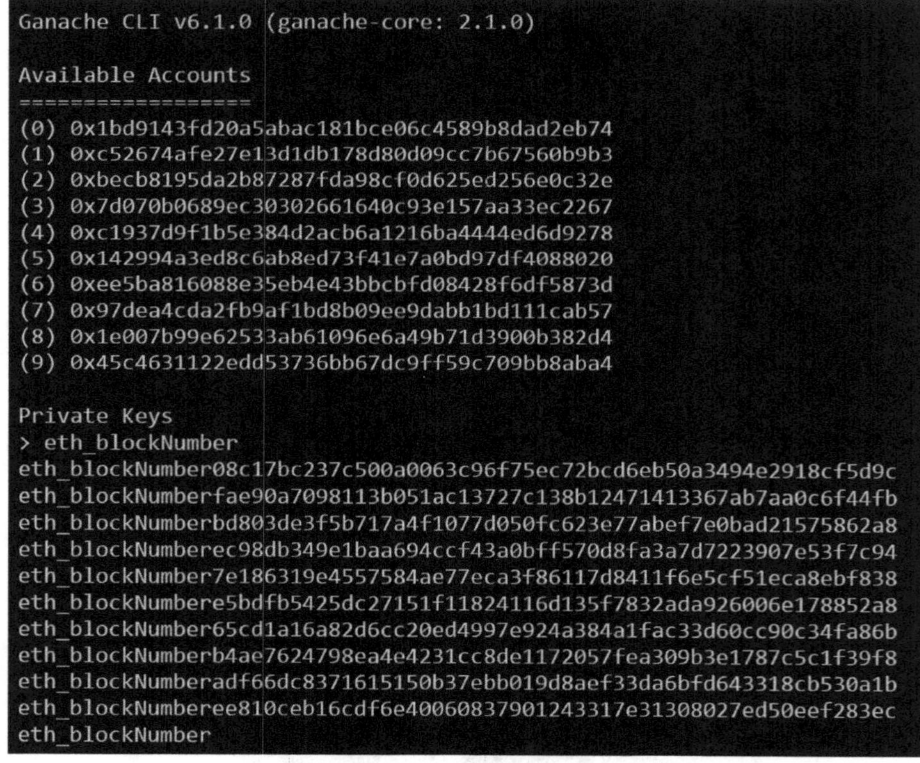

Ganache CLI v6.1.0 (ganache-core: 2.1.0)
Available Accounts
==================
(0) 0x1bd9143fd20a5abac181bce06c4589b8dad2eb74
(1) 0xc52674afe27e13d1db178d80d09cc7b67560b9b3
(2) 0xbecb8195da2b87287fda98cf0d625ed256e0c32e
(3) 0x7d070b0689ec30302661640c93e157aa33ec2267
(4) 0xc1937d9f1b5e384d2acb6a1216ba4444ed6d9278
(5) 0x142994a3ed8c6ab8ed73f41e7a0bd97df4088020
(6) 0xee5ba816088e35eb4e43bbcbfd08428f6df5873d
(7) 0x97dea4cda2fb9af1bd8b09ee9dabb1bd111cab57
(8) 0x1e007b99e62533ab61096e6a49b71d3900b382d4
(9) 0x45c4631122edd53736bb67dc9ff59c709bb8aba4
Private Keys
> eth_blockNumber
eth_blockNumber08c17bc237c500a0063c96f75ec72bcd6eb50a3494e2918cf5d9c
eth_blockNumberfae90a7098113b051ac13727c138b12471413367ab7aa0c6f44fb
eth_blockNumberbd803de3f5b717a4f1077d050fc623e77abef7e0bad21575862a8
eth_blockNumberec98db349e1baa694ccf43a0bff570d8fa3a7d7223907e53f7c94
eth_blockNumber7e186319e4557584ae77eca3f86117d8411f6e5cf51eca8ebf838
eth_blockNumbere5bdfb5425dc27151f11824116d135f7832ada926006e178852a8
eth_blockNumber65cd1a16a82d6cc20ed4997e924a384a1fac33d60cc90c34fa86b
eth_blockNumberb4ae7624798ea4e4231cc8de1172057fea309b3e1787c5c1f39f8
eth_blockNumberadf66dc8371615150b37ebb019d8aef33da6bfd643318cb530a1b
eth_blockNumberee810ceb16cdf6e40060837901243317e31308027ed50eef283ec
eth_blockNumber

In our Truffle project, `truffle.js` defined `7545` as the default port number. We need to update the port number to `8545` to match with the Ganache port number, as follows:

```
module.exports = {
  networks: {
    development: {
      host: "127.0.0.1",
      port: 8545,
      network_id: "*" // Match any network id
    }
  }
};
```

Deploying a smart contract

As you might have noticed, two migration-related files were created by the previous command, `Migrations.sol` and `1_initial_migration.js`. `Migrations.sol` stores a number that corresponds to the last applied "migration" script. When you add a new contract and deploy the contract, the number of the last deployment in stores will increase. After the contract has run once, it will not run again. The numbering convention is `x_script_name.js`, with x starting at 1, that is `1_initial_migration.js`. Your new contracts would typically come in scripts starting at `2_...`.

In our case, we will add a new migration contract to deploy `CrowdFunding`. Let's create a file called `2_deploy_contracts.js`.

`CrowdFunding.sol` defines the constructor as follows:

```
constructor (address _owner, uint _minimumToRaise, uint _durationProjects,
        string _name, string _website)
```

To deploy a contract, with optional constructor arguments, you can call the truffle deploy function, `deployer.deploy(contract, args..., options)`.

We will use the first account given to us by Ganache as the owner account, as follows:

```
var CrowdFunding = artifacts.require("./CrowdFunding.sol");
module.exports = (deployer, network, accounts) => {
  const ownerAddress = accounts[0];
  deployer.deploy(CrowdFunding, ownerAddress, 30, 60, "smartchart",
"smartchart.tech");
}
```

Let's deploy the smart contract to our network. Run the `truffle` command, as follows:

```
truffle migrate
```

The following screenshot displays the result for running the command for `truffle migrate`:

```
Using network 'development'.

Running migration: 1_initial_migration.js
  Deploying Migrations...
  ... 0xd2e9f62dbbcfca6da38b09e5bbb82a4019fa09e87d00ebfd45416b757f676c48
  Migrations: 0x77ab1ca444797a862e1555e418c73b7aeaf03b90
Saving successful migration to network...
  ... 0xc221d7e60f0f46d0fc7c5f00281918b7837f5a412d9149600c11a8d5f57c525c
Saving artifacts...
Running migration: 2_deploy_contracts.js
  Deploying CrowdFunding...
  ... 0x1b163aac8f62076039081896afb0b897bdae27470536485546f474a2ef4f2084
  CrowdFunding: 0x9e24eea74f385e95cf61df1d5f441108a6715356
Saving successful migration to network...
  ... 0xeef193b79458260af8abdc2ab8d8f96d88e672a8a963e24efa7f965aa4389e9a
Saving artifacts...
```

This deploys our crowdfunding smart contract in a local Ganache blockchain environment.

To bring your local node server up, run the following command, which will bring up the pet store page in our browser:

```
npm run dev
```

Writing a campaign decentralized application

We just deployed our smart contract on our local Ganache blockchain environment. Now, we will start to write UI code to trigger smart contract functions through an RPC call. The source code for this chapter is available here:

`https://github.com/PacktPublishing/Blockchain-Quick-Start-Guide/tree/master/Chapter04/CrowdFunding.`

Selecting a web3 provider

When we load a web page, we need to connect to a web3 provider. If you have already installed a provider such as MetaMask, you can use your correct provider option, as follows:

```
App.web3Provider = web3.currentProvider;
```

In our crowdfunding example, for the sake of simplicity, we will directly connect to our local Ganache server, as follows:

```
App.web3Provider = new
Web3.providers.HttpProvider('http://localhost:8545');
```

Loading account information

To load accounts, we define a drop-down menu with empty content, as follows:

```
<div class="form-group">
                <label for="exampleFormControlSelect1">Accounts</label>
                <select class="form-control" id="accts">
                </select>
              </div>
```

When we load the page, we will use `web3.eth.accounts` to get all 10 default accounts. Notice that the first account has an ether balance of 99.84; this is because we used the first account as the owner account to deploy the contract and burned some gas as the transaction fee, as shown in the following code:

```
    web3.eth.accounts.forEach( function(e){
        $('#accts').append($('<option>', {
            value:e,
            text : e + " (" +web3.fromWei(web3.eth.getBalance(e), "ether")
+ " ether)"
        }));
})
```

Once the accounts are loaded, it will be displayed as follows:

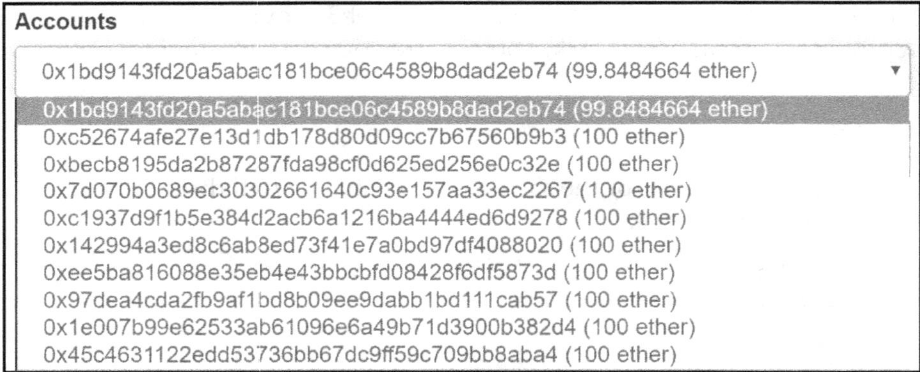

Loading project information

In crowdfunding, we defined a project struct that contains fundraising information, as follows:

```
struct Project {
        address addr;
        string name;
        string website;
        uint totalRaised;
        uint minimumToRaise;
        uint currentBalance;
        uint deadline;
        uint completeAt;
        Status status;
    }
```

Let's define some related information in HTML, for example:

```
<table class="table table-hover table-striped">
                 <tbody>
                   <tr>
                     <th scope="row">address</th>
                     <td><span class="text-info" id="address"></span
</td>
                   </tr>
                   <tr>
                     <th scope="row">name</th>
                     <td><span class="text-info" id="name"></span></td>
```

```
                    </tr>
                    <tr>
                        <th scope="row">website</th>
                        <td><span class="text-info"
id="website"></span></td>
                    </tr>
                    <tr>
                        <th scope="row">totalRaised</th>
                        <td><span class="text-info"
id="totalRaised"></span></td>
...
                  </tbody>
                </table>
```

The `CrowdFunding.deployed()` function will create an instance of `CrowdFunding` that represents the default address managed by `CrowdFunding`. The code here shows us how to display project information:

```
      App.contracts.CrowdFunding.deployed().then(function(instance) {
        crowdFundingInstance = instance;
        return crowdFundingInstance.project();
      }).then(function(projectInfo) {
          $("#address").text(projectInfo[0].toString());
          $("#name").text(projectInfo[1]);
          $("#website").text(projectInfo[2]);
          $("#totalRaised").text(projectInfo[3].toString());
          ..
          if(projectInfo[6].toString().length>0) {
            var deadline = new
Date(Number(projectInfo[6].toString())*1000);
            deadlineDate = moment(deadline).format("YYYY-MM-DD h:mm:ss");
            $("#deadline").text(deadlineDate);
          }
          if(projectInfo[7].toString().length>0 &&
projectInfo[7].toString()!='0') {
            console.log(projectInfo[7].toString());
            var completeAt = new
Date(Number(projectInfo[7].toString())*1000);
            completeAtDate = moment(completeAt).format("YYYY-MM-DD h:mm:ss");
            $("#completeAt").text(completeAtDate);
          }
      }).catch(function(error) {
..
      });
```

The result will be displayed as follows:

	Project
address	0x1bd9143fd20a5abac181bce06c4589b8dad2eb74
name	smartchart
website	smartchart.tech
totalRaised	0
minimumToRaise	3000000000000000000
currentBalance	0
deadline	2018-11-15 7:29:49
completeAt	
status	Fundraising

Handling the fund function

To raise funds, we need to call the fund function, which is defined in our crowdfunding smart contract. In our web page, we use the HTML range input slider component to contribute fund amounts, as follows:

```
<form id="fund-form" method="post" role="form" style="display: block;">
                                      <div class="form-group row">
                                          <div class="row">
                                              <div class="col-lg-12">
                                                  <input type="range"
name="ageInputName" id="ageInputId" value="0" min="1" max="100"
oninput="ageOutputId.value = ageInputId.value">
                                                  <div style="display:
inline;"><output name="ageOutputName" id="ageOutputId">0</output>
<span>ether</span></div>
                                              </div>
                                            </div>
                                       </div>
                                      <div class="form-group">
                                        <div class="row">
```

```
                                    <div class="col-lg-12">
                                        <button type="button"
id="fundBtn" class="btn btn-primary pull-left">Submit</button>
                                    </div>
                                </div>
                            </div>
                        </form>
```

The `Crowdfunding fund` function is a payable fallback function; therefore, we need to pass `msg.sender` and `msg.value` from the UI to call it, as follows.

```
    function fund() public atStage(Status.Fundraising) payable {
        contributions.push(
            Contribution({
                addr: msg.sender,
                amount: msg.value
                })
            );
......
}
```

You can define the sending address and value parameters as follows:

```
  handleFund: function(event) {
    event.preventDefault();
    var fundVal =  $('#ageOutputId').val();
    var selectAcct = $('#accts').find(":selected").val();
    $("#displayMsg").html("");
    App.contracts.CrowdFunding.deployed().then(function(instance) {
      return instance.fund({ from: selectAcct, value:web3.toWei(fundVal,
"ether"), gas:3500000});
    }).then(function(result) {
      App.loadProject();
    }).catch(function(err) {
      console.error(err);
      $("#displayMsg").html(err);
    });
  },
```

Once we get the result back, we will call the `loadProject` function to refresh the project information. We can see that the current balance fund increased, as shown in the following screenshot:

checkGoalReached

Once the funding goal is reached, the crowdfunding owner will collect of the all funds by running the `checkGoalReached` method.

The HTML is just a simple button, as shown in the following code:

```
<button type="button" id="checkGoal" class="btn btn-
success">CheckGoal</button>
```

Similar to the fund function, we call the smart contract in JavaScript using the following code:

```
instance.checkGoalReached({ from: selectAcct, gas:3500000});
```

Here is the detailed logic:

```
handleCheckGoal: function(event) {
  event.preventDefault();
  $("#displayMsg").html("");
  var selectAcct = $('#accts').find(":selected").val();
  App.contracts.CrowdFunding.deployed().then(function(instance) {
    return instance.checkGoalReached({ from: selectAcct, gas:3500000});
  }).then(function(result) {
    App.loadProject();
  }).catch(function(err) {
    console.error(err);
    $("#displayMsg").html(err);
  });
},
```

The result will display as follows:

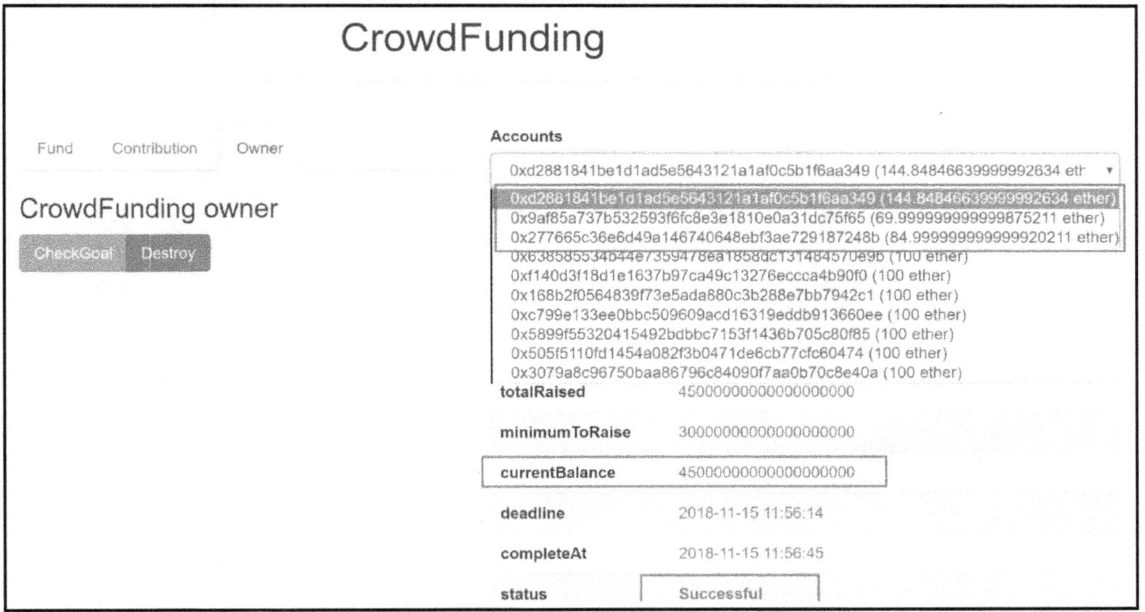

If you followed the whole example and run this step, congratulations! You are now able to write and run a crowdfunding DApp.

Summary

In this chapter, we learned DApp basics and we now understand the web3.js API. By running Ganache as our local Ethereum environment, we could use the Truffle development tool to create a crowdfunding project and write a DApp component. Finally, we deployed and launched the crowdfunding DApp. In the next chapter, we will start to explore the most popular enterprise blockchain—Hyperledger Fabric.

5
Exploring an Enterprise Blockchain Application Using Hyperledger Fabric

the previous chapter, we discussed the Ethereum blockchain. Ethereum is a public blockchain; anyone can read the blockchain data and make legitimate changes. Anyone can write a new block into the chain. Ethereum is fully autonomous and is not controlled by anyone. The smart contract is written in Solidity, as a nearly Turing complete language, that can run on the **Ethereum virtual machine** (**EVM**) to execute various transactions. Developers can build and deploy **decentralized applications** (**DApps**) using these smart contracts. Ether is a cryptocurrency in Ethereum, and acts as fuel for every operation in Ethereum, including executing smart contracts, DApps, transactions, and so on. However, this is not the only way to build a blockchain.

Blockchains that require an access control layer built into the blockchain nodes to read restricted information on the blockchain can be created. This will limit the number of participants in the network who can transact in the consensus mechanism of the blockchain's network. This kind of blockchain is called a permissioned blockchain.

The differences between public and permissioned blockchains are shown in the following table:

	Permissionless	**Permissioned**
Public	Everyone can read the transaction data. Everyone can validate a transaction in the block. • **Speed**: Poor • **Consensus**: Proof-of-Work • **Blockchain**: Bitcoin, Ethereum • **Token**: Needed	Everyone can read the transaction data. Only predefined users can validate a transaction. • **Speed**: Good • **Consensus**: Proof-of-Work • **Blockchain**: Ethereum after Casper • **Token**: Needed
Private	Only predefined users can read transaction data. Only predefined users can validate a transaction. • **Speed**: Good • **Consensus**: **Federated byzantine agreement** (**FBA**) • **Token**: Not needed	Only predefined users can read transaction data. Only entitled users can validate a transaction. • **Speed**: Good • **Consensus**: **Practical Byzantine Fault Tolerance Algorithm** (**PBFT**) • **Blockchain**: Hyperledger Fabric • **Token**: Not needed

Hyperledger Fabric is one such private permissioned blockchains. In this chapter, we will discuss the Hyperledger Fabric blockchain.

Hyperledger Fabric is an open source enterprise blockchain technology. The project was initially contributed by IBM and digital asset. Hyperledger Fabric is one of the blockchain projects hosted by the Linux foundation. The smart contract in Hyperledger Fabric is called *chaincode*, which defines the business logic for Fabric applications. The modular architecture design enables Fabric to support high degrees of confidentiality, resiliency, flexibility, and scalability. The components in Fabric, such as consensus and membership services, can be plug and play.

In this chapter, we will cover the following topics:

- Key concepts in Hyperledger Fabric
- Core component model
- Setting up a Hyperledger Fabric environment
- Write a chaincode
- Configuring Hyperledger Fabric

Key concepts in Hyperledger Fabric

If you want to use Hyperledger Fabric effectively, you have to understand its key concepts. This includes ledger, chaincode, and channel.

Ledger

The ledger is the sequenced, immutable, entire historical record of all state transactions. All the transactions that are performed will be added to the ledger. We can find the entire transaction history for each channel. A fabric blockchain ledger has two types of data—a world state and a blockchain transaction ledger. The world state, which is stored stored in a database, LevelDB, is the default database. The state data is mutable. It has a version number that keeps incrementally updated when the state changes. On the other hand, the ledger data is immutable, and is stored as a file. It records transaction data block information, which contains a sequence of transactions. Each block's header includes a hash of the block's transactions, as shown in the following diagram:

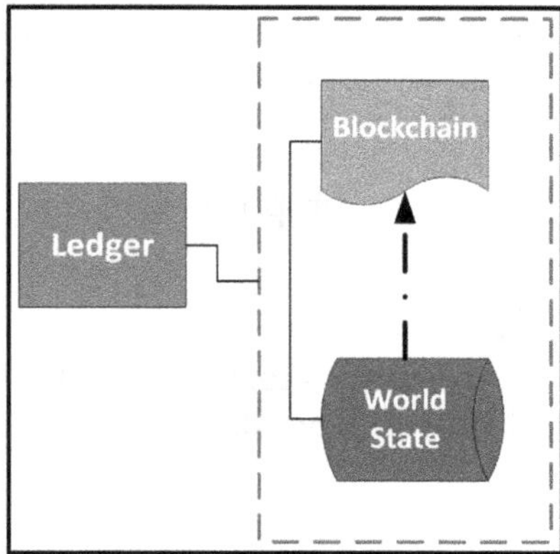

Chaincode

Chaincode is a program (or programs) that runs on top of the Hyperledger Fabric blockchain to implement the business logic of how applications interact with the ledger. It is currently written in Go, Node.js, and eventually will be written in other programming languages, such as Java, that implement a prescribed interface. When a transaction is invoked, it triggers the chaincode that decides what state change should be applied to the ledger. Chaincode is typically considered a **smart contract**. A state created by chaincode is restricted in scope to that chaincode and can't be accessed directly by another chaincode.

Channel

In a Hyperledger network, the channel is a communication private *subnet* that's used to connect a number of peer nodes (member). All transactions executed in the channel are confidential to members who participant in the related channel. Each channel has its own separate ledger, and the ledgers are shared and stored in each peer on that channel.

Core component model

To run Hyperledger Fabric, we need a few main components; these are a **Membership Service Provider** (**MSP**), Fabric CA, peers, and an ordering service. We need to understand exactly how they work and the way to collect them.

Peers

The peers are the physical layer where the ledger data is stored and the chaincode is processed. A blockchain network is comprised primarily of a set of peer nodes. Every peer maintains its own copy of the shared ledger and is certified by a single MSP. The peer can have two roles: endorsing nodes or committing nodes.

The endorsing node processes transaction proposals and it returns the signed result to the client.

The ordering service sends a block of transactions to the committing node. The committing node validates if the data is in a consistent state. Once verified, it commits the transaction in the ledger and updates the world state in store data.

Membership service provider (MSP)

MSP is a pluggable interface that aims to offer an abstraction of a membership credentials architecture, and provides cryptographic mechanisms and protocols to issue and validate certificates and user authentication. MSP abstraction provides the following:

- Concrete identity format
- User credential validation
- User credential revocation
- Signature generation and verification

Clients and peers use these credentials to authenticate their transactions and process results. The MSP is installed on each channel peer to ensure secured transactions for each channel.

Certificate authority (CA)

Fabric CA is used to manage identity services to participants including nodes, users, and all members of organizations on the network. It manages the different types of certificates required to run the blockchain. Every transaction that happens in the blockchain must be signed using a certificate. Fabric CA provides the following:

- Registration of identities with roles or integration with an existing LDAP or **Active Directory** (**AD**). This compromises the user registry, which is used to fetch the identities of the mentioned roles.
- Issuance of **enrolment certificates** (**ECerts**).
- Issuance of **transaction certificates** (**TCerts**).
- Certificate renewal and revocation.

Ordering service

The ordering service, or orderer, builds a shared communication channel between clients and peers. It atomically broadcasts messages containing transactions to peers to be committed. All peers receive the same block of transactions in the same order. The ordering service orders transactions on a first come, first serve basis for all channels on the network. After the transaction is ordered, the records of the committed are grouped and assigned as part of the block for that communication channel.

Hyperledger Fabric basic transaction flow

We have learned the basic concepts and components of Hyperledger Fabric. In this section, we will explore the basic transaction flow in greater detail. We have outlined the high-level transaction flow as follows:

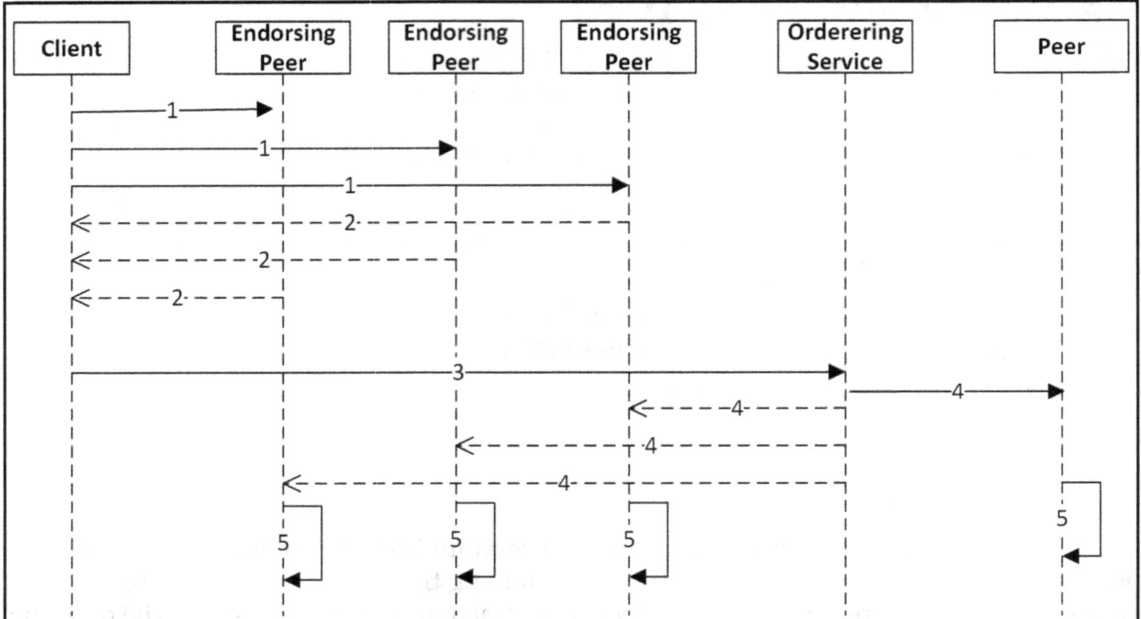

The detailed steps are as follows:

1. The client signs and initiates a transaction proposal to one or more endorsers for execution.
2. Endorsing peers verify the signature, simulate the proposal, and execute the operation on the specified chaincode. The endorser produces a writeset and a readset of keys during the simulation. The endorsing peers send back the signed proposal responses (endorsements) to the client.
3. The client collects and verifies the endorsements until the endorsement policy of the chaincode is satisfied with producing the same result. The client then creates a transaction and passes it to the ordering service.

4. The ordering service creates blocks and delivers the blocks of transactions to all peers on the channel. The peers validate transactions to ensure that the endorsement policy is satisfied and to ensure that there have been no changes to the ledger state since the proposal response was generated by the transaction execution.
5. After successful validation, the block is committed to the ledger. Once the ledger blockchain is updated, the world state is updated too. The client can detect the status change via event handling.

Issuance claim

In this section, we will explore and implement an issuance claim use case.

No one wants to have an insurance claim, but when things do go wrong and accidents happen, this may result in financial losses. These losses will be covered by your insurance policy. The traditional insurance claims process has stayed the same for decades, as there are a number of key issues in the process, including false claims, fraud detection, slow and complex claims processing, human error, undesirable customer experience, and inefficient information flows in reinsurance.

With blockchain, the transaction record in the ledger is immutable and the state data can only be updated when all parties agree. The record in the blockchain can be shared in real time. This allows insurers to move quickly, as most of the required information for claims verification can be processed in no time. Insurers can track the use of asset data in the blockchain. The paperwork can be eliminated and customers can submit claims via a web application.

Let's take a look at the insurance claim process, as shown in the following screenshot. For demonstration purposes, we simplified the claim process, as it can be much more complex in a real-world use case:

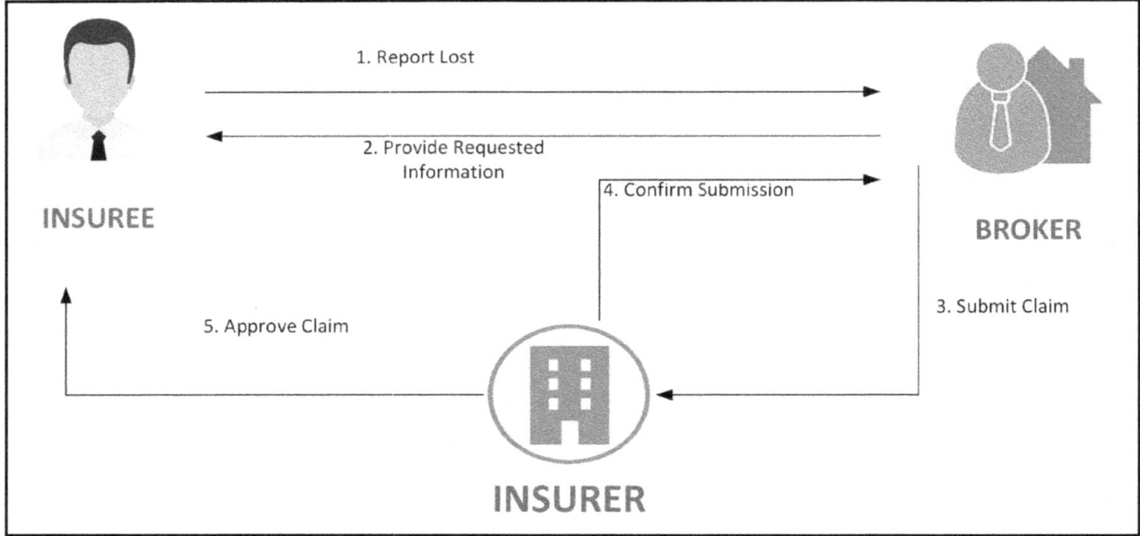

For the preceding process, the steps are as follows:

1. An insuree reports a claim to a broker
2. A broker provides requested information
3. A broker submits a claim to an issuer
4. An issuer confirms the claim
5. An issuer process and approves the claim

Setting up a Hyperledger Fabric environment

So far, we have learned about the key concepts of Hyperledger Fabric. In this section, we will set up a Hyperledger Fabric development environment. Before continuing with the installation steps, let's take a look at the prerequisites for fabric installation.

Installation prerequisites

The following are the prerequisites for installing the required development tools.

Ubuntu Linux 14.04 / 16.04 LTS (both 64-bit), or macOS 10.12	Docker Engine: Version 17.03 or higher
Docker-Compose: Version 1.8 or higher	Node: 8.9 or higher (note version 9 is not supported)
npm: v5.x	git: 2.9.x or higher
Python: 2.7.x	

We will use Ubuntu for our development environment. We can download the prerequisites using the following commands:

```
curl -O https://hyperledger.github.io/composer/latest/prereqs-ubuntu.sh
chmod u+x prereqs-ubuntu.sh
./prereqs-ubuntu.sh
```

It may prompt for your password, since it uses `sudo` during its execution.

Installing Hyperledger Fabric

Create and navigate to the project folder called `insurance-claim`, as follows:

```
mkdir ~/insurance-claim && cd ~/insurance-claim
```

Enter the following command to install the Hyperledger Fabric platform-specific binaries:

```
curl -sSL
https://raw.githubusercontent.com/hyperledger/fabric/release-1.3/scripts/bo
otstrap.sh | bash
```

After this executes, it downloads the following platform-specific binaries in the `bin` folder, which is located under the `fabric-samples` folder. You can set `fabric-samples/bin` as a `PATH` variable as follows:

```
export PATH=<path to download location>/bin:$PATH
```

We also provide `bootstrap-hyperledger.sh` from the code files in this book, and you can download it from the Packt site. Once you get the file, you can directly run the following script, and it will create a bin folder and download binaries to this folder:

```
===> List out hyperledger docker images
hyperledger/fabric-ca          1.3.0-rc1    784b38dab5ba    5 days ago     244MB
hyperledger/fabric-ca          latest       784b38dab5ba    5 days ago     244MB
hyperledger/fabric-tools       1.3.0-rc1    693f6ae1c95c    5 days ago     1.5GB
hyperledger/fabric-tools       latest       693f6ae1c95c    5 days ago     1.5GB
hyperledger/fabric-ccenv       1.3.0-rc1    04415e10d1f2    5 days ago     1.38GB
hyperledger/fabric-ccenv       latest       04415e10d1f2    5 days ago     1.38GB
hyperledger/fabric-orderer     1.3.0-rc1    4f5d3e993eb8    5 days ago     145MB
hyperledger/fabric-orderer     latest       4f5d3e993eb8    5 days ago     145MB
hyperledger/fabric-peer        1.3.0-rc1    3286d6b8fe00    5 days ago     151MB
hyperledger/fabric-peer        latest       3286d6b8fe00    5 days ago     151MB
hyperledger/fabric-zookeeper   0.4.12       bca71b814159    12 days ago    1.39GB
hyperledger/fabric-zookeeper   latest       bca71b814159    12 days ago    1.39GB
hyperledger/fabric-kafka       0.4.12       58b901c762ea    12 days ago    1.4GB
hyperledger/fabric-kafka       latest       58b901c762ea    12 days ago    1.4GB
hyperledger/fabric-couchdb     0.4.12       fe8d64d1233c    12 days ago    1.45GB
hyperledger/fabric-couchdb     latest       fe8d64d1233c    12 days ago    1.45GB
```

These components will be part of our Hyperledger Fabric network.

Writing chaincode

Chaincode is similar to a *smart contract*. It defines and executes the business logic invoked by authorized participants in a specific network. A chaincode is written in Go or Node.js. In our example, we will use Go.

There are many IDEs and tools to support Golang. Here are some popular IDEs that work great with Golang.

Development tools

There are various tools that support Go development. Some popular IDEs are listed in the following sections.

LiteIDE

LiteIDE is an open source Go IDE that was directly designed for Golang. There are a bunch of useful features available for Go developers, including a configurable code editor, customized build commands, many building options, and Golang support.

JetBrains Gogland

Gogland has a powerful built-in autocomplete engine, errors detection, code refactoring tools, and more.

Visual Studio Code

You can install Go extension in Visual Studio Code. It provides code hints and the ability to debug code.

In this chapter, we will use LiteIDE to develop our chaincode. Follow the official LiteIDE installation guide to set up your local IDE environment, which is available from the following link:

`https://github.com/visualfc/liteide/blob/master/liteidex/deploy/welcome/en/install.md`.

Chaincode key concept and APIs

There are three important functions in Fabric chaincode: `Init`, and `Invoke`, `Query`. Every chaincode program must implement the chaincode interface, as follows:

```
type Chaincode interface {
    Init(stub ChaincodeStubInterface) pb.Response
    Invoke(stub ChaincodeStubInterface) pb.Response
}
```

`Init()` is called when the application initializes its internal data for other chaincode functions to use. It is triggered when a chaincode receives an instantiate or upgrade transaction.

When the application client proposes an update or query transaction, the `Invoke();` function is called.

`Query()` is called when a chaincode queries a chaincode state. Hyperledger Fabric uses LevelDB (key/value store) as the default database to store world;state data. You can use a key to get the current ledger state data. The query function reads the value of a chaincode state by passing in the key value.

The shim package provides APIs for the chaincode to access its state variables, transaction context, and call other chaincodes.

`ChaincodeStubInterface` is one of the important interfaces. It provides various functions that let you query, update, and delete assets in the ledger. These are as follows:

`GetState(key string) ([]byte, error)`	`GetState` returns the value of the specified key from the ledger
`PutState(key string, value []byte) error`	`PutState` puts the specified key and value into the transaction's writeset as a data-write proposal
`DelState(key string) error`	`DelState` records the specified key to be deleted in the writeset of the transaction proposal

Defining an issuance claim

Let's write a chaincode. Open LiteIDE and create a new file called `claimcontract.go`, as follows:

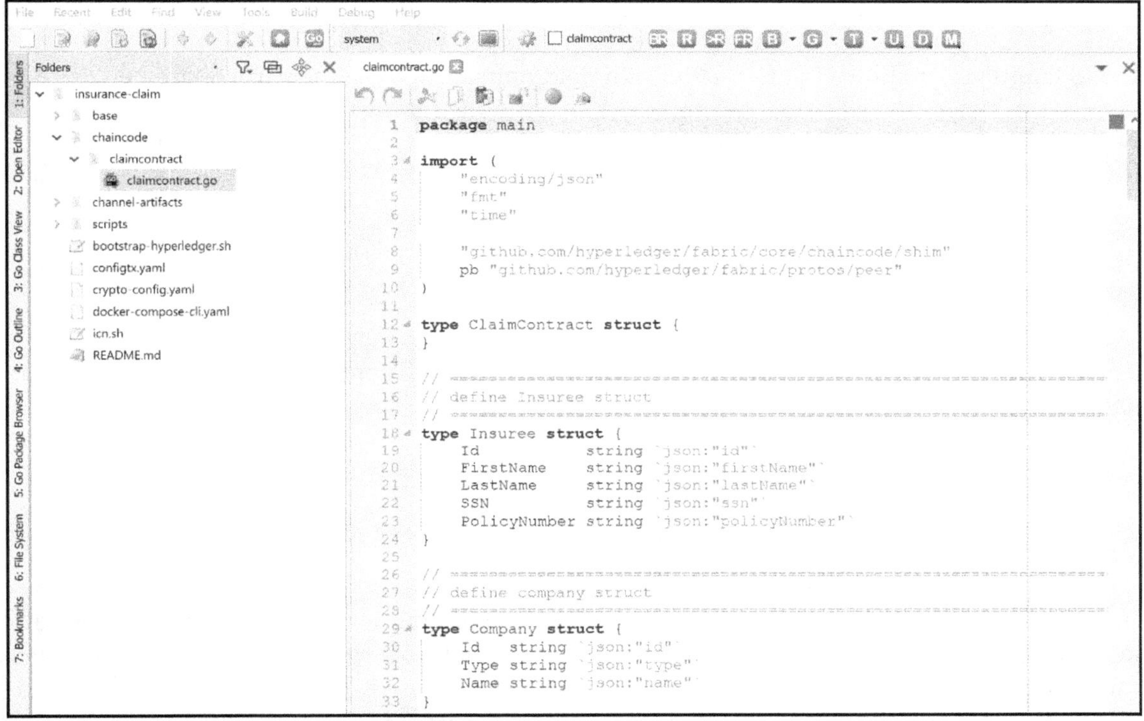

In the insurance claim use case analysis, we analysed the participants in the issuance claim process. There are three participants for whom we need to define a chaincode: insuree, broker, and insurer, as shown in the following example:

```
type Insuree struct {
        Id           string `json:"id"`
        FirstName    string `json:"firstName"`
        LastName     string `json:"lastName"`
        SSN          string `json:"ssn"`
        PolicyNumber string `json:"policyNumber"`
}
```

In `Insuree`, we define `Id`, `firstname`, `LastName`, `SSN`, and `policyNumber`.

In Go language, it allows the first letter of a field name as to be either uppercase or lowercase. When we need an exported field to be public for any piece of code to use it, it needs to be a capitalized letter. You can use encoding in the JSON package to unmarshal data into struct, which defines the field name in JSON as the `firstName` key, as shown in the following format:

```
type Member struct {
  Name string `json:"member_name"`
}
```

The broker and insurers data models are similar and only different in type. We define them as follows:

```
type Company struct {
         Id   string `json:"id"`
         Type string `json:"type"`
         Name string `json:"name"`
}
```

In the issuance claim process, `Insuree` initializes a claim request. The claim document will keep track of each step of the process in the blockchain. It records all necessary information, including status, user claim description, `insueeId`, `brokerId`, `insurerId`, process time at each step, and comments entered from an authorized party, as shown in the following example:

```
type Claim struct {
         Id         string `json:"id"`         //the fieldtags are needed to
keep case from bouncing around
         Desc       string `json:"desc"`       //claim description
         Status     string `json:"status"`     //status of claim
         InsureeId  string `json:"insureeId"`  //InsureeId
         BrokerId   string `json:"brokerId"`   //BrokerId
         InsurerId  string `json:"insurerId"`  //InsurerId
         Comment    string `json:"comment"`    //comment
         ProcessAt  string `json:"processAt"`  //processAt
}
```

Initializing the chaincode

Next, we'll implement the `Init` function. `Init()` allows the chaincode to initialize the insuree data to start the claim request. In our case, we will set up and register the insuree person information, as follows:

```
func (c *ClaimContract) Init(stub shim.ChaincodeStubInterface) pb.Response
{
        args := stub.GetStringArgs()
        if len(args) != 5 {
                return shim.Error("Incorrect arguments. Expecting a key
and a value")
        }
        insureeId := args[0]
        firstName := args[1]
        lastName := args[2]
        ssn := args[3]
        policyNumber := args[4]
        insureeData := Insuree{
                Id:             insureeId,
                FirstName:      firstName,
                LastName:       lastName,
                SSN:            ssn,
                PolicyNumber: policyNumber}
        insureeBytes, _ := json.Marshal(insureeData)
        err := stub.PutState(insureeId, insureeBytes)
        if err != nil {
                return shim.Error(fmt.Sprintf("Failed to create asset:
%s", args[0]))
        }
        return shim.Success(nil)
}
```

`ChaincodeStubInterface.GetStringArg` gets the input arguments. It expects that the length of the arguments should be 5. With all required insurer data, we build Insurer JSON data and encode it to JSON byte strings –`json.Marshal(insureeData`. Then, we store the key and the value on the ledger. If all went well, it returns a `peer.Response` object with success to Fabric's `client.c`.

Invoking the chaincode

To trigger the invoke function, you can call the name of the chaincode application function and pass `shim.ChaincodeStubInterface` as the signature. In the insurance claim case, we defined several functions to support our use case, for example:

`AddCompany`, `ReportLost`, `RequestedInfo`, `SubmitClaim`, `ConfirmClaimSubmission`, `ApproveClaim`.

We also defined a query to keep track of the current claim request and `getHistory` to get all of the historical claim transaction records, as follows:

```
func (c *ClaimContract) Invoke(stub shim.ChaincodeStubInterface)
pb.Response {
         function, args := stub.GetFunctionAndParameters()
         if function == "AddCompany" {
                 return c.AddCompany(stub, args)
         } else if function == "ReportLost" {
                 return c.ReportLost(stub, args)
         } else if function == "RequestedInfo" {
                 return c.RequestedInfo(stub, args)
         } else if function == "SubmitClaim" {
                 return c.SubmitClaim(stub, args)
         } else if function == "ConfirmClaimSubmission" {
                 return c.ConfirmClaimSubmission(stub, args)
         } else if function == "ApproveClaim" {
                 return c.ApproveClaim(stub, args)
         } else if function == "query" {
                 return c.query(stub, args)
         } else if function == "getHistory" {
                 return c.getHistory(stub, args)
         }


         return shim.Error("Invalid function name")
}
```

AddCompany

`AddCompany` is similar to how we added insuree at the Init step. Chaincode can register brokers and insurers through this function. The company type can be a *broker* or *insurer*, as follows:

```
func (c *ClaimContract) AddCompany(stub shim.ChaincodeStubInterface, args
[]string) pb.Response {
```

```
        id := args[0]
        name := args[1]
        companyType := args[2]
        companyData := Company{
                Id:   id,
                Type: companyType,
                Name: name}
        companyBytes, _ := json.Marshal(companyData)
        stub.PutState(id, companyBytes)
        return shim.Success(companyBytes)
}
```

ReportLost

In this step, the insuree reports the lost item to the broker with all the claim information. This function also records the current system process time at the `processAt` field. `currentts.Format(2006-01-02 15:04:05)` is a Go custom format; it will convert the current time into YYYY-MM-dd hh:mm:ss format, as shown in the following example:

```
func (c *ClaimContract) ReportLost(stub shim.ChaincodeStubInterface, args
[]string) pb.Response {
        claimId := args[0]
        desc := args[1]
        insureeId := args[2]
        brokerId := args[3]
        currentts := time.Now()
        processAt := currentts.Format("2006-01-02 15:04:05")
        //initialized claim
        claimData := Claim{
                Id:        claimId,
                Desc:      desc,
                Status:    "ReportLost",
                InsureeId: insureeId,
                BrokerId:  brokerId,
                InsurerId: "",
                Comment:   "",
                ProcessAt: processAt}
        claimBytes, _ := json.Marshal(claimData)
        stub.PutState(claimId, claimBytes)
        return shim.Success(claimBytes)
}
```

RequestedInfo

After the insuree reports a loss, the next step is for the broker to return `RequestedInfo`, as follows:

```
func (c *ClaimContract) RequestedInfo(stub shim.ChaincodeStubInterface,
args []string) pb.Response {
         return c.UpdateClaim(stub, args, "RequestedInfo")
}
func (c *ClaimContract) UpdateClaim(stub shim.ChaincodeStubInterface, args
[]string, currentStatus string) pb.Response {
         claimId := args[0]
         comment := args[1]
         claimBytes, err := stub.GetState(claimId)
         claim := Claim{}
         err = json.Unmarshal(claimBytes, &claim)
         if err != nil {
                 return shim.Error(err.Error())
         }
         if currentStatus == "RequestedInfo" && claim.Status !=
"ReportLost" {
                 claim.Status = "Error"
                 fmt.Printf("Claim is not initialized yet")
                 return shim.Error(err.Error())
         } else if currentStatus == "SubmitClaim" && claim.Status !=
"RequestedInfo" {
                 claim.Status = "Error"
                 fmt.Printf("Claim must be in RequestedInfo status")
                 return shim.Error(err.Error())
         } else if currentStatus == "ConfirmClaimSubmission" &&
claim.Status != "SubmitClaim" {
                 claim.Status = "Error"
                 fmt.Printf("Claim must be in Submit Claim status")
                 return shim.Error(err.Error())
         } else if currentStatus == "ApproveClaim" && claim.Status !=
"ConfirmClaimSubmission" {
                 claim.Status = "Error"
                 fmt.Printf("Claim must be in Confirm Claim Submission
status")
                 return shim.Error(err.Error())
         }
         claim.Comment = comment
         if currentStatus == "RequestedInfo" {
                 insurerId := args[2]
                 claim.InsurerId = insurerId
         }
         currentts := time.Now()
         claim.ProcessAt = currentts.Format("2006-01-02 15:04:05")
```

```
        claim.Status = currentStatus
        claimBytes0, _ := json.Marshal(claim)
        err = stub.PutState(claimId, claimBytes0)
        if err != nil {
                return shim.Error(err.Error())
        }
        return shim.Success(claimBytes0)
}
```

Since the remaining process functions are quite similar, we define `UpdateClaim` as a common function to share with the remaining steps.

The `UpdateClaim` function first gets `claimId` and the current participant comment from input arguments. It then queries and gets a claim from the blockchain to decode the claim data and turns it into a JSON string—`json.Unmarshal(claimBytes, &claim)`.

Before updating the claim content, it will validate the input claim status and make sure it is on the expected step. If all goes well, we will update the claim status, participant comment, and process time.

Finally, we update the claim data with `claimId` as a key on the ledger.

SubmitClaim, ConfirmClaimSubmission, ApproveClaim

Submitting, confirming, and approving the claim are very similar to `RequestedInfo`, and these steps are called by the `UpdateClaim` function. Only the comment, status, and process time values are different.

Query

Queries are how you read data from the ledger. The query function is used to query the chaincode's state. As we put claim data in the ledger with `claimId`, in order to read the current claim, we call `GetState`, passing `claimId` as key, as follows:

```
func (c *ClaimContract) query(stub shim.ChaincodeStubInterface, args
[]string) pb.Response {
        var ENIITY string
        var err error
        if len(args) != 1 {
                return shim.Error("Incorrect number of arguments. Expected
ENIITY Name")
```

```
        }
        ENIITY = args[0]
        Avalbytes, err := stub.GetState(ENIITY)         if err != nil {
                jsonResp := "{\"Error\":\"Failed to get state for " +
ENIITY + "\"}"
                return shim.Error(jsonResp)
        }
        if Avalbytes == nil {
                jsonResp := "{\"Error\":\"Nil order for " + ENIITY + "\"}"
                return shim.Error(jsonResp)
        }
        return shim.Success(Avalbytes)
}
```

getHistory

As its name indicates, the `gethistory` function reads a claim of all historical values records for a key, as well as the `TxId` and claim value.

We first define the `AuditHistory` struct, which has `TxId` and value. `GetHistoryForKey` returns the list of results with `resultsIterator`, which contains all historical transaction records. We iterate through these records and add them to an array of `AuditHistory`. Later, we convert it to JSON byte and send the data back as a response, as follows:

```
func (c *ClaimContract) getHistory(stub shim.ChaincodeStubInterface, args
[]string) pb.Response {
        type AuditHistory struct {
                TxId  string `json:"txId"`
                Value Claim  `json:"value"`
        }
        var history []AuditHistory
        var claim Claim
        if len(args) != 1 {
                return shim.Error("Incorrect number of arguments.
Expecting 1")
        }
        claimId := args[0]
        fmt.Printf("- start getHistoryForClaim: %s\n", claimId)


        // Get History
        resultsIterator, err := stub.GetHistoryForKey(claimId)
        if err != nil {
                return shim.Error(err.Error())
        }
        defer resultsIterator.Close()
```

```
        for resultsIterator.HasNext() {
                historyData, err := resultsIterator.Next()
                if err != nil {
                        return shim.Error(err.Error())
                }
                var tx AuditHistory
                tx.TxId = historyData.TxId
                json.Unmarshal(historyData.Value, &claim)
                tx.Value = claim              //copy claim over
                history = append(history, tx) //add this tx to the list
        }
        fmt.Printf("- getHistoryForClaim returning:\n%s", history)


        //change to array of bytes
        historyAsBytes, _ := json.Marshal(history) //convert to array of
bytes
        return shim.Success(historyAsBytes)
}
```

This covers our issuance claim chaincode. We will learn about Hyperledger Fabric configuration in the next section.

Configuring Hyperledger Fabric

There are three entities in the insurance claim network—insuree, broker, and insurer. All of these participants will register in Fabric as a peer node. The following table describes the three peer roles and MSP information:

User ID	Role	Organization MSP ID
user_001	INSUREE	Org1MSP
broker_001	BROKER	Org2MSP
insurer_001	INSURER	Org3MSP

We have one insuree who joins the organization with MSP ID org1, one broker who joins the organization with MSP ID org2, and one insurer who joins the organization with MSP ID org3. For bootstrapping the fabric network, we need to first generate crypto material for all three components that we need to run.

Generating the certificate

We need to define `crypto-config.yaml` and use the cryptogen tool to generate the certificates for each peer. Cryptogen is available in the tools image. `crypto-config.yaml` contains the following information:

- **OrdererOrgs**: Definition of organizations managing orderer nodes
- **PeerOrgs**: Definition of organizations managing peer nodes

OrdererOrgs contains the following information about the ordered node in the cluster:

- **Name**: Name of the orderer
- **Domain**: Domain URL for orderer; in our case, it is ic.com
- **Hostname**: Hostname for the orderer

Here is an example:

```
OrdererOrgs:
  - Name: Orderer
    Domain: ic.com
    Specs:

      - Hostname: orderer
```

PeerOrgs contains the following information about the peer node in the cluster:

- **Name**: Name of the organization; we have three different orgs : `Org1`, `Org2`, and `Org3`
- **Template count**: Number of peer nodes for an organization
- **Users count**: Number of users for an organization

Here is an example:

```
PeerOrgs:
  # --------------------------------------------------------------------
----
  # Org1
  # --------------------------------------------------------------------
----
  - Name: Org1
    Domain: org1.ic.com
    Template:
      Count: 2
    Users:
```

```
      Count: 1
  # ---------------------------------------------------------------------------
----
  # Org2
  # ---------------------------------------------------------------------------
----
  - Name: Org2
    Domain: org2.ic.com
    Template:
      Count: 2
    Users:
      Count: 1
  # ---------------------------------------------------------------------------
----
  # Org3
  # ---------------------------------------------------------------------------
----
  - Name: Org3
    Domain: org3.ic.com
    Template:
      Count: 2
    Users:
      Count: 1
```

The following is the command thats used to generate the crypto material:

```
cryptogen generate --config=./crypto-config.yaml
```

After running the cryptogen tool, you should see the following output in the console:

```
###############################################################
##### Generate certificates using cryptogen tool #########
###############################################################

org1.ic.com
org2.ic.com
org3.ic.com
```

Generating an orderer genesis block

After generating the certificate, the next step in the process is to generate the orderer genesis block. The `configtxgen` command allows users to create and inspect channel config. The `configtxgen` tool's output is largely controlled by the content of `configtx.yaml`, as follows:

```
Profiles:
    ICOrgsOrdererGenesis:
        Orderer:
            <<: *OrdererDefaults
            Organizations:
                - *OrdererOrg
        Consortiums:
            InsuranceClaimConsortium:
                Organizations:
                    - *Org1
                    - *Org2
                    - *Org3
    ICOrgsChannel:
        Consortium: InsuranceClaimConsortium
        Application:
            <<: *ApplicationDefaults
            Organizations:
                - *Org1
                - *Org2
                - *Org3
Organizations:
    - &OrdererOrg
        Name: OrdererOrg
        ID: OrdererMSP
        MSPDir: crypto-config/ordererOrganizations/ic.com/msp
    - &Org1
        Name: Org1MSP
        ID: Org1MSP
        MSPDir: crypto-config/peerOrganizations/org1.ic.com/msp
        AnchorPeers:
            - Host: peer0.org1.ic.com
              Port: 7051
    - &Org2
        Name: Org2MSP
        ID: Org2MSP
        MSPDir: crypto-config/peerOrganizations/org2.ic.com/msp
        AnchorPeers:
            - Host: peer0.org2.ic.com
              Port: 7051
    - &Org3
```

```
        Name: Org3MSP
        ID: Org3MSP
        MSPDir: crypto-config/peerOrganizations/org3.ic.com/msp


        AnchorPeers:
            - Host: peer0.org3.ic.com
              Port: 7051
Orderer: &OrdererDefaults
    OrdererType: solo
    Addresses:
        - orderer.ic.com:7050
    BatchTimeout: 2s
    BatchSize:
        MaxMessageCount: 10
        AbsoluteMaxBytes: 20 MB
        PreferredMaxBytes: 512 KB
    Kafka:
        Brokers:
            - 127.0.0.1:9092
    Organizations:
Application: &ApplicationDefaults


    Organizations:
```

We defined three organizations in the `Organizations` section of the `configtx` file; we specified each organization name, `ID`, `MSPDir`, and `AnchorPeers`. `MSPDir` describes cryptogen generated output MSP directories. `AnchorPeers` points to the peer node's host and port. It updates transactions in order to enable communication between peers of different organizations and finds all active participants of the channel, as follows:

```
configtxgen -profile ICOrgsOrdererGenesis -outputBlock ./channel-
artifacts/genesis.block
```

An output similar to the following will be displayed on the console:

```
#################################################################
#########  Generating Orderer Genesis block ##############
#################################################################
2018-10-03 18:32:04.833 UTC [common/configtx/tool] main -> INFO 001 Loading configuration
2018-10-03 18:32:04.860 UTC [common/configtx/tool] doOutputBlock -> INFO 002 Generating genesis block
2018-10-03 18:32:04.862 UTC [common/configtx/tool] doOutputBlock -> INFO 003 Writing genesis block
```

Generating a channel configuration transaction

`configtxgen` writes a channel creation transaction to `channel.tx` by executing a channel configuration transaction, as follows:

```
configtxgen -profile ICOrgsChannel -outputCreateChannelTx ./channel-artifacts/channel.tx -channelID icchannel
```

An output similar to the following will be displayed on the console:

```
#################################################################
### Generating channel configuration transaction 'channel.tx' ###
#################################################################
2018-10-03 18:32:04.884 UTC [common/configtx/tool] main -> INFO 001 Loading configuration
2018-10-03 18:32:04.887 UTC [common/configtx/tool] doOutputChannelCreateTx -> INFO 002 Generating new channel configtx
2018-10-03 18:32:04.888 UTC [common/configtx/tool] doOutputChannelCreateTx -> INFO 003 Writing new channel tx
```

Output for executing channel configuration transaction

Overview of Hyperledger Fabric Docker composer configuration files

Hyperledger Fabric utilizes Docker compose to define fabric application services. The `docker-compose-cli.yaml` service section is the place for defining all peer services and related containers. Hyperledger Fabric's *first-network* provides a `.yaml` template to help you quickly start to create yaml files from scratch:

`https://github.com/hyperledger/fabric-samples/tree/release-1.2/first-network.`

In `docker-compose-cli.yaml`, we define the following information:

- `networks`: Definition of the blockchain network name. In our case, it is `icn`
- `services`: Definition of all peer services and related Docker containers
- `cli`: Definition of the Cli container that is used to replace the SDK client, and environment variables for Docker compose command-line behavior

Here is an example configuration for the network and service section:

```
networks:
  icn:
services:
  orderer.ic.com:
    extends:
      file:   base/docker-compose-base.yaml
      service: orderer.ic.com
```

```
    container_name: orderer.ic.com
    networks:
      - icn
  peer0.org1.ic.com:
    container_name: peer0.org1.ic.com
    extends:
      file:  base/docker-compose-base.yaml
      service: peer0.org1.ic.com
    networks:
      - icn
```

As you can see, there is a file extension directory: `base/docker-compose-base.yaml`. Docker compose supports sharing common configuration for individual services with the *extends* field. We will discuss more on `docker-compose-base.yaml` later.

Here is an example of configuration for `cli` section:

```
cli:
    container_name: cli
    image: hyperledger/fabric-tools
    tty: true
    environment:
      - GOPATH=/opt/gopath
      - CORE_VM_ENDPOINT=unix:///host/var/run/docker.sock
      - CORE_LOGGING_LEVEL=DEBUG
      - CORE_PEER_ID=cli
      - CORE_PEER_ADDRESS=peer0.org1.ic.com:7051
      - CORE_PEER_LOCALMSPID=Org1MSP
      - CORE_PEER_TLS_ENABLED=true
      -
CORE_PEER_TLS_CERT_FILE=/opt/gopath/src/github.com/hyperledger/fabric/peer/
crypto/peerOrganizations/org1.ic.com/peers/peer0.org1.ic.com/tls/server.crt
      -
CORE_PEER_TLS_KEY_FILE=/opt/gopath/src/github.com/hyperledger/fabric/peer/c
rypto/peerOrganizations/org1.ic.com/peers/peer0.org1.ic.com/tls/server.key
      -
CORE_PEER_TLS_ROOTCERT_FILE=/opt/gopath/src/github.com/hyperledger/fabric/p
eer/crypto/peerOrganizations/org1.ic.com/peers/peer0.org1.ic.com/tls/ca.crt
      -
CORE_PEER_MSPCONFIGPATH=/opt/gopath/src/github.com/hyperledger/fabric/peer/
crypto/peerOrganizations/org1.ic.com/users/Admin@org1.ic.com/msp
    working_dir: /opt/gopath/src/github.com/hyperledger/fabric/peer
    command: /bin/bash -c './scripts/script.sh ${CHANNEL_NAME} ${DELAY};
sleep $TIMEOUT'
    #for mapping the directories that are being used in the environment
configurations
    volumes:
        - /var/run/:/host/var/run/
```

```
        - ./chaincode/:/opt/gopath/src/github.com/chaincode
        - ./crypto-
config:/opt/gopath/src/github.com/hyperledger/fabric/peer/crypto/
        -
./scripts:/opt/gopath/src/github.com/hyperledger/fabric/peer/scripts/
        - ./channel-
artifacts:/opt/gopath/src/github.com/hyperledger/fabric/peer/channel-
artifacts
    depends_on:
      - orderer.ic.com
      - peer0.org1.ic.com
      - peer0.org2.ic.com
      - peer0.org3.ic.com
    networks:
      - icn
```

The `docker-compose` tool uses the `docker-compose-cli.yaml` file to initialize the fabric runtime environment. Blow are some of the most common commands you will use when using `docker-compose-cli.yaml` file:

`TTY`	TTY basically means *a console*, and we set it as true.
`Image`	Points to the fabric-tools image directory.
`Environment`	Specifies environment variables, for example, GOPATH, a TLS-related file location generated by the cryptogen tool.
`working_dir`	Sets the working directory for the peer.
`command`	Specifies the command that is issued when the container starts.
`volumes`	Maps the directories that are being used in the environment configurations.
`depends_on`	Starts services in dependency order.

It then generates four fabric-peer transaction node containers, one fabric-order orderer node container, and one fabric-tools cli container.

Fabric project directory structure

In our Fabric sample first-network, the project structure is similar to the following:

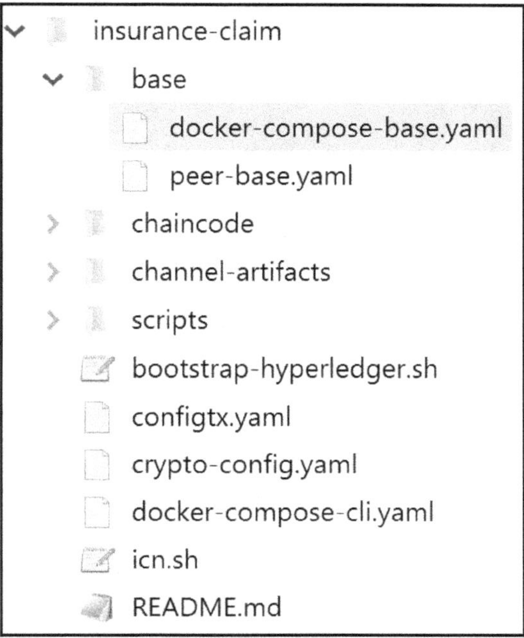

As we discussed previously, the `docker-compose-cli.yaml` service extends from `base/docker-compose-base.yaml`. There are two file base directories: `peer-base.yaml` and `docker-compose-base.yaml`.

Docker-compose-base.yaml

This file contains the base configurations, including each peer and orderer container environment and port number. This defines the overall topology of the insurance claim network, as follows:

```
services:
  orderer.ic.com:
    container_name: orderer.ic.com
    image: hyperledger/fabric-orderer
    environment:
      - ORDERER_GENERAL_LOGLEVEL=debug
      - ORDERER_GENERAL_LISTENADDRESS=0.0.0.0
      - ORDERER_GENERAL_GENESISMETHOD=file
      -
ORDERER_GENERAL_GENESISFILE=/var/hyperledger/orderer/orderer.genesis.block
      - ORDERER_GENERAL_LOCALMSPID=OrdererMSP
      - ORDERER_GENERAL_LOCALMSPDIR=/var/hyperledger/orderer/msp
```

```
      # enabled TLS
      - ORDERER_GENERAL_TLS_ENABLED=true
      -
ORDERER_GENERAL_TLS_PRIVATEKEY=/var/hyperledger/orderer/tls/server.key
      -
ORDERER_GENERAL_TLS_CERTIFICATE=/var/hyperledger/orderer/tls/server.crt
      - ORDERER_GENERAL_TLS_ROOTCAS=[/var/hyperledger/orderer/tls/ca.crt]
    working_dir: /opt/gopath/src/github.com/hyperledger/fabric
    command: orderer
    volumes:
    - ../channel-
artifacts/genesis.block:/var/hyperledger/orderer/orderer.genesis.block
    - ../crypto-
config/ordererOrganizations/ic.com/orderers/orderer.ic.com/msp:/var/hyperle
dger/orderer/msp
    - ../crypto-
config/ordererOrganizations/ic.com/orderers/orderer.ic.com/tls/:/var/hyperl
edger/orderer/tls
    ports:
      - 7050:7050


  peer0.org1.ic.com:
    container_name: peer0.org1.ic.com
    extends:
      file: peer-base.yaml
      service: peer-base
    environment:
      - CORE_PEER_ID=peer0.org1.ic.com
      - CORE_PEER_ADDRESS=peer0.org1.ic.com:7051
      - CORE_PEER_GOSSIP_EXTERNALENDPOINT=peer0.org1.ic.com:7051
      - CORE_PEER_LOCALMSPID=Org1MSP
    volumes:
        - /var/run/:/host/var/run/
        - ../crypto-
config/peerOrganizations/org1.ic.com/peers/peer0.org1.ic.com/msp:/etc/hyper
ledger/fabric/msp
        - ../crypto-
config/peerOrganizations/org1.ic.com/peers/peer0.org1.ic.com/tls:/etc/hyper
ledger/fabric/tls
    ports:
      - 7051:7051
      - 7053:7053
.....
```

Peer-base.yaml

This file defines peer network configuration for the insurance claim `docker-compose-base.yaml`, as follows:

```
services:
  peer-base:
    image: hyperledger/fabric-peer
    environment:
      - CORE_VM_ENDPOINT=unix:///host/var/run/docker.sock
      - CORE_VM_DOCKER_HOSTCONFIG_NETWORKMODE=${COMPOSE_PROJECT_NAME}_icn
      - CORE_LOGGING_LEVEL=DEBUG
      - CORE_PEER_TLS_ENABLED=true
      - CORE_PEER_GOSSIP_USELEADERELECTION=true
      - CORE_PEER_GOSSIP_ORGLEADER=false
      - CORE_PEER_PROFILE_ENABLED=true
      - CORE_PEER_TLS_CERT_FILE=/etc/hyperledger/fabric/tls/server.crt
      - CORE_PEER_TLS_KEY_FILE=/etc/hyperledger/fabric/tls/server.key
      - CORE_PEER_TLS_ROOTCERT_FILE=/etc/hyperledger/fabric/tls/ca.crt
    working_dir: /opt/gopath/src/github.com/hyperledger/fabric/peer
    command: peer node start
```

The command in the peer gets the peer to install the system chaincode and other configurations.

We have an overview of the critical Hyperledger Fabric configuration files, so let's start our insurance claim network using the following code:

```
      - CORE_PEER_TLS_KEY_FILE=/etc/hyperledger/fabric/tls/server.key
      - CORE_PEER_TLS_ROOTCERT_FILE=/etc/hyperledger/fabric/tls/ca.crt
    working_dir: /opt/gopath/src/github.com/hyperledger/fabric/peer
    command: peer node start
```

Starting the Hyperledger Fabric network

Now, it is time to bring up our Hyperledger Fabric network. We will use Docker commands to kick off the new Docker compose initially:

```
docker-compose -f docker-compose-cli.yaml up
```

The Docker container will trigger the command defined in `docker-compose-cli.yaml`, as follows:

```
command: /bin/bash -c './scripts/script.sh
```

`script.sh` is a script that contains a series of instructions to fabric deployment and test commands. We also define some business-specific shell script functions in `utils.sh`.

Creating a channel

First, we need to create a channel to build a genesis block. Run the following command:

```
peer channel create -o orderer.ic.com:7050 -c icchannel -f ./channel-artifacts/channel.tx
```

This command reads a genesis block from `channel.tx` that is then used to join the channel and creates the icchannel channel. Here is the result on the console:

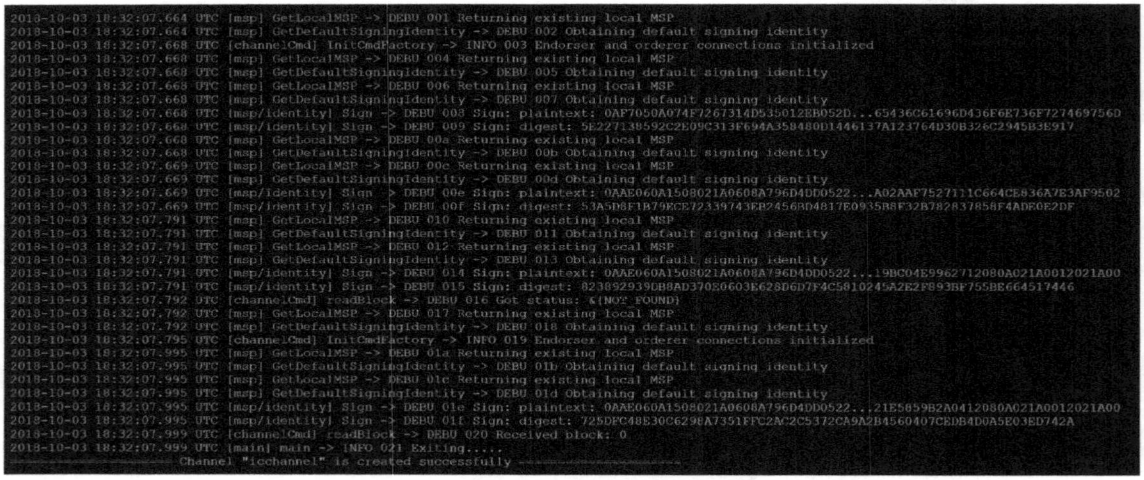

```
2018-10-03 18:32:07.664 UTC [msp] GetLocalMSP -> DEBU 001 Returning existing local MSP
2018-10-03 18:32:07.664 UTC [msp] GetDefaultSigningIdentity -> DEBU 002 Obtaining default signing identity
2018-10-03 18:32:07.668 UTC [channelCmd] InitCmdFactory -> INFO 003 Endorser and orderer connections initialized
2018-10-03 18:32:07.668 UTC [msp] GetLocalMSP -> DEBU 004 Returning existing local MSP
2018-10-03 18:32:07.668 UTC [msp] GetDefaultSigningIdentity -> DEBU 005 Obtaining default signing identity
2018-10-03 18:32:07.668 UTC [msp] GetLocalMSP -> DEBU 006 Returning existing local MSP
2018-10-03 18:32:07.668 UTC [msp] GetDefaultSigningIdentity -> DEBU 007 Obtaining default signing identity
2018-10-03 18:32:07.668 UTC [msp/identity] Sign -> DEBU 008 Sign: plaintext: 0AF7050A074F7267314D535012EB052D...65436C61696D436F6E736F727469756D
2018-10-03 18:32:07.668 UTC [msp/identity] Sign -> DEBU 009 Sign: digest: 5E227138592C2E09C313F694A358480D1446137A123764D30B326C2945B3E917
2018-10-03 18:32:07.668 UTC [msp] GetLocalMSP -> DEBU 00a Returning existing local MSP
2018-10-03 18:32:07.668 UTC [msp] GetDefaultSigningIdentity -> DEBU 00b Obtaining default signing identity
2018-10-03 18:32:07.669 UTC [msp] GetLocalMSP -> DEBU 00c Returning existing local MSP
2018-10-03 18:32:07.669 UTC [msp] GetDefaultSigningIdentity -> DEBU 00d Obtaining default signing identity
2018-10-03 18:32:07.669 UTC [msp/identity] Sign -> DEBU 00e Sign: plaintext: 0AAE060A1508021A0608A796D4DD0522...A02AAF7527111C664CE836A7E3AF9502
2018-10-03 18:32:07.669 UTC [msp/identity] Sign -> DEBU 00f Sign: digest: 53A5D8F1B79ECE72339743EB2456BD4817E0935B8F32B782837858F4ADE0E2DF
2018-10-03 18:32:07.791 UTC [msp] GetLocalMSP -> DEBU 010 Returning existing local MSP
2018-10-03 18:32:07.791 UTC [msp] GetDefaultSigningIdentity -> DEBU 011 Obtaining default signing identity
2018-10-03 18:32:07.791 UTC [msp] GetLocalMSP -> DEBU 012 Returning existing local MSP
2018-10-03 18:32:07.791 UTC [msp] GetDefaultSigningIdentity -> DEBU 013 Obtaining default signing identity
2018-10-03 18:32:07.791 UTC [msp/identity] Sign -> DEBU 014 Sign: plaintext: 0AAE060A1508021A0608A796D4DD0522...19BC04E9962712080A021A0012021A00
2018-10-03 18:32:07.791 UTC [msp/identity] Sign -> DEBU 015 Sign: digest: 823892939DB8AD370E0603E628D6D7F4C5810245A2E2F893BF755BE664517446
2018-10-03 18:32:07.792 UTC [channelCmd] readBlock -> DEBU 016 Got status: &{NOT_FOUND}
2018-10-03 18:32:07.792 UTC [msp] GetLocalMSP -> DEBU 017 Returning existing local MSP
2018-10-03 18:32:07.792 UTC [msp] GetDefaultSigningIdentity -> DEBU 018 Obtaining default signing identity
2018-10-03 18:32:07.795 UTC [channelCmd] InitCmdFactory -> INFO 019 Endorser and orderer connections initialized
2018-10-03 18:32:07.995 UTC [msp] GetLocalMSP -> DEBU 01a Returning existing local MSP
2018-10-03 18:32:07.995 UTC [msp] GetDefaultSigningIdentity -> DEBU 01b Obtaining default signing identity
2018-10-03 18:32:07.995 UTC [msp] GetLocalMSP -> DEBU 01c Returning existing local MSP
2018-10-03 18:32:07.995 UTC [msp] GetDefaultSigningIdentity -> DEBU 01d Obtaining default signing identity
2018-10-03 18:32:07.995 UTC [msp/identity] Sign -> DEBU 01e Sign: plaintext: 0AAE060A1508021A0608A796D4DD0522...21E5859B2A0412080A021A0012021A00
2018-10-03 18:32:07.995 UTC [msp/identity] Sign -> DEBU 01f Sign: digest: 725DFC48E30C6298A7351FFC2AC2C5372CA9A2B4560407CEDB4D0A5E03ED742A
2018-10-03 18:32:07.999 UTC [channelCmd] readBlock -> DEBU 020 Received block: 0
2018-10-03 18:32:07.999 UTC [main] main -> INFO 021 Exiting.....
===================== Channel "icchannel" is created successfully =====================
```

Output for the console that joins and creates the channel

Joining channels

After the ordering service creates the channel, we can add the peers to the channel, as follows:

```
peer channel join -b icchannel.block
```

Here is the result on the console:

```
===================== peer.org1 joined on the channel "icchannel" =====================

CORE_PEER_TLS_ROOTCERT_FILE=/opt/gopath/src/github.com/hyperledger/fabric/peer/crypto/peerOrganizations/org2.ic.com/peers/peer0.org2.ic.com/tls/ca.crt
CORE_PEER_TLS_KEY_FILE=/opt/gopath/src/github.com/hyperledger/fabric/peer/crypto/peerOrganizations/org1.ic.com/peers/peer0.org1.ic.com/tls/server.key
CORE_PEER_LOCALMSPID=Org2MSP
CORE_VM_ENDPOINT=unix:///host/var/run/docker.sock
CORE_PEER_TLS_CERT_FILE=/opt/gopath/src/github.com/hyperledger/fabric/peer/crypto/peerOrganizations/org1.ic.com/peers/peer0.org1.ic.com/tls/server.crt
CORE_PEER_TLS_ENABLED=true
CORE_PEER_MSPCONFIGPATH=/opt/gopath/src/github.com/hyperledger/fabric/peer/crypto/peerOrganizations/org2.ic.com/users/Admin@org2.ic.com/msp
CORE_PEER_ID=cli
CORE_LOGGING_LEVEL=DEBUG
CORE_PEER_ADDRESS=peer0.org2.ic.com:7051
2018-10-03 18:32:11.149 UTC [msp] GetLocalMSP -> DEBU 001 Returning existing local MSP
2018-10-03 18:32:11.149 UTC [msp] GetDefaultSigningIdentity -> DEBU 002 Obtaining default signing identity
2018-10-03 18:32:11.152 UTC [channelCmd] InitCmdFactory -> INFO 003 Endorser and orderer connections initialized
2018-10-03 18:32:11.153 UTC [msp/identity] Sign -> DEBU 004 Sign: plaintext: 0AF4060A5B08011A0B08AB96D4DD0510...5C12AB7F74DB1A080A000A000A000A00
2018-10-03 18:32:11.153 UTC [msp/identity] Sign -> DEBU 005 Sign: digest: 3C95B5655B8AFABA1BECC836D0F756E6D05181763F483F205E5E464EB72B9140
2018-10-03 18:32:11.187 UTC [channelCmd] executeJoin -> INFO 006 Peer joined the channel!
2018-10-03 18:32:11.187 UTC [main] main -> INFO 007 Exiting.....
===================== peer.org2 joined on the channel "icchannel" =====================

CORE_PEER_TLS_ROOTCERT_FILE=/opt/gopath/src/github.com/hyperledger/fabric/peer/crypto/peerOrganizations/org3.ic.com/peers/peer0.org3.ic.com/tls/ca.crt
CORE_PEER_TLS_KEY_FILE=/opt/gopath/src/github.com/hyperledger/fabric/peer/crypto/peerOrganizations/org1.ic.com/peers/peer0.org1.ic.com/tls/server.key
CORE_PEER_LOCALMSPID=Org3MSP
CORE_VM_ENDPOINT=unix:///host/var/run/docker.sock
CORE_PEER_TLS_CERT_FILE=/opt/gopath/src/github.com/hyperledger/fabric/peer/crypto/peerOrganizations/org1.ic.com/peers/peer0.org1.ic.com/tls/server.crt
CORE_PEER_TLS_ENABLED=true
CORE_PEER_MSPCONFIGPATH=/opt/gopath/src/github.com/hyperledger/fabric/peer/crypto/peerOrganizations/org3.ic.com/users/Admin@org3.ic.com/msp
CORE_PEER_ID=cli
CORE_LOGGING_LEVEL=DEBUG
CORE_PEER_ADDRESS=peer0.org3.ic.com:7051
2018-10-03 18:32:14.237 UTC [msp] GetLocalMSP -> DEBU 001 Returning existing local MSP
2018-10-03 18:32:14.237 UTC [msp] GetDefaultSigningIdentity -> DEBU 002 Obtaining default signing identity
2018-10-03 18:32:14.240 UTC [channelCmd] InitCmdFactory -> INFO 003 Endorser and orderer connections initialized
2018-10-03 18:32:14.240 UTC [msp/identity] Sign -> DEBU 004 Sign: plaintext: 0AF4060A5B08011A0B08AE96D4DD0510...5C12AB7F74DB1A080A000A000A000A00
2018-10-03 18:32:14.240 UTC [msp/identity] Sign -> DEBU 005 Sign: digest: E1E4B7FBD3FD006FD48E8C5DF7BEAB0436609C8D0C792707F8D84BF943532DF6
2018-10-03 18:32:14.267 UTC [channelCmd] executeJoin -> INFO 006 Peer joined the channel!
2018-10-03 18:32:14.267 UTC [main] main -> INFO 007 Exiting.....
===================== peer.org3 joined on the channel "icchannel" =====================
```

Adding peers to the channel

We can see that `peer0.org1`, `peer0.org2`, and `peer0.org3` are joined in the channel.

Updating the anchor

The last operation that we need to complete before we start to interact with our issuance claim network is to update the anchor peers. Anchor peers receive and broadcast transaction updates to the other peers in the organization. Anchor peers are searchable in the network. Therefore, any peer registered as an anchor peer can be discovered by an order peer or any other peer, for example:

```
peer channel update -f ./channel-artifacts/Org1MSPanchors.tx -c icchannel -
o orderer.ic.com:7050 --tls true --cafile $ORDERER_CA
```

Here is the console output for this step:

```
2018-10-03 18:32:20.432 UTC [main] main -> INFO 010 Exiting.....
-------------------- Updates Anchor peer.org2 on the channel "icchannel" --------------------

CORE_PEER_TLS_ROOTCERT_FILE=/opt/gopath/src/github.com/hyperledger/fabric/peer/crypto/peerOrganizations/org3.ic.com/peers/peer0.org3.ic.com/tls/ca.crt
CORE_PEER_TLS_KEY_FILE=/opt/gopath/src/github.com/hyperledger/fabric/peer/crypto/peerOrganizations/org1.ic.com/peers/peer0.org1.ic.com/tls/server.key
CORE_PEER_LOCALMSPID=Org3MSP
CORE_VM_ENDPOINT=unix:///host/var/run/docker.sock
CORE_PEER_TLS_CERT_FILE=/opt/gopath/src/github.com/hyperledger/fabric/peer/crypto/peerOrganizations/org1.ic.com/peers/peer0.org1.ic.com/tls/server.crt
CORE_PEER_TLS_ENABLED=true
CORE_PEER_MSPCONFIGPATH=/opt/gopath/src/github.com/hyperledger/fabric/peer/crypto/peerOrganizations/org3.ic.com/users/Admin@org3.ic.com/msp
CORE_PEER_ID=cli
CORE_LOGGING_LEVEL=DEBUG
CORE_PEER_ADDRESS=peer0.org3.ic.com:7051
2018-10-03 18:32:23.486 UTC [msp] GetLocalMSP -> DEBU 001 Returning existing local MSP
2018-10-03 18:32:23.486 UTC [msp] GetDefaultSigningIdentity -> DEBU 002 Obtaining default signing identity
2018-10-03 18:32:23.489 UTC [channelCmd] InitCmdFactory -> INFO 003 Endorser and orderer connections initialized
2018-10-03 18:32:23.489 UTC [msp] GetLocalMSP -> DEBU 004 Returning existing local MSP
2018-10-03 18:32:23.489 UTC [msp] GetDefaultSigningIdentity -> DEBU 005 Obtaining default signing identity
2018-10-03 18:32:23.489 UTC [msp] GetLocalMSP -> DEBU 006 Returning existing local MSP
2018-10-03 18:32:23.489 UTC [msp] GetDefaultSigningIdentity -> DEBU 007 Obtaining default signing identity
2018-10-03 18:32:23.489 UTC [msp/identity] Sign -> DEBU 008 Sign: plaintext: 0AF7050A074F7267334D535012EB052D...2A0641646D696E732A0641646D696E73
2018-10-03 18:32:23.489 UTC [msp/identity] Sign -> DEBU 009 Sign: digest: 269EC668E364EF2EC0167CFE6938F24D61B57FCFF54FEDF267A8F6DA29757D3A
2018-10-03 18:32:23.489 UTC [msp] GetLocalMSP -> DEBU 00a Returning existing local MSP
2018-10-03 18:32:23.489 UTC [msp] GetDefaultSigningIdentity -> DEBU 00b Obtaining default signing identity
2018-10-03 18:32:23.489 UTC [msp] GetLocalMSP -> DEBU 00c Returning existing local MSP
2018-10-03 18:32:23.489 UTC [msp] GetDefaultSigningIdentity -> DEBU 00d Obtaining default signing identity
2018-10-03 18:32:23.489 UTC [msp/identity] Sign -> DEBU 00e Sign: plaintext: 0AAE060A1508021A0608B796D4DD0522...14C6DACB5C8F8A884B5FC28E4702FB1B
2018-10-03 18:32:23.489 UTC [msp/identity] Sign -> DEBU 00f Sign: digest: 968615F7B4DE75CF7ABA6DA73CDA55E6CB13C2B4C3380D7BEA05C05107BDF8D8
2018-10-03 18:32:23.518 UTC [main] main -> INFO 010 Exiting.....
-------------------- Updates Anchor peer.org3 on the channel "icchannel" --------------------
```

Getting discovered by an order peer or any other peer

Installing chaincode

After the previous steps, we are almost ready to use our issuance claim blockchain application. However first, we need to install `claimcontract.go` chaincode on our network, as follows:

```
peer chaincode install -n iccc -v 1.0 -l golang -p
github.com/chaincode/claimcontract
```

We will see the output of the preceding command:

Installing chaincode to our network

Instantiating the chaincode

After installing the chaincode, we need to instantiate it. As we discussed previously, we will onboard insuree in the `init()` chaincode. Therefore, we need to pass the required arguments to create an insuree participant, as follows:

```
peer chaincode instantiate -o orderer.ic.com:7050 -C icchannel -n iccc -l
golang -v 1.0 -c '{"Args":[ "user_001","John","Smith",
"9999","4394497111/1"]}' -P "OR    ('Org1MSP.member'
```

Here is the output for this step:

Creating an insuree participant

We query the insuree to verify that the record has been created in the blockchain, as follows:

```
peer chaincode query -C $CHANNEL_NAME -n iccc -c
'{"Args":["query","user_001"]}'
```

We can see from this output that the insuree (`user_001`) was added in our blockchain:

```
========== Querying on peerPEER0.org1 on channel 'icchannel'... =======
Attempting to Query peerPEER0.org1 ...3 secs
Attempting to Query peerPEER0.org1 ...6 secs
Attempting to Query peerPEER0.org1 ...9 secs
Attempting to Query peerPEER0.org1 ...13 secs
Attempting to Query peerPEER0.org1 ...16 secs
Attempting to Query peerPEER0.org1 ...19 secs
Attempting to Query peerPEER0.org1 ...22 secs

2018-10-03 18:33:01.253 UTC [msp] GetLocalMSP -> DEBU 001 Returning existing local MSP
2018-10-03 18:33:01.253 UTC [msp] GetDefaultSigningIdentity -> DEBU 002 Obtaining default signing identity
2018-10-03 18:33:01.253 UTC [chaincodeCmd] checkChaincodeCmdParams -> INFO 003 Using default escc
2018-10-03 18:33:01.253 UTC [chaincodeCmd] checkChaincodeCmdParams -> INFO 004 Using default vscc
2018-10-03 18:33:01.254 UTC [msp/identity] Sign -> DEBU 005 Sign: plaintext: 0AFF060A6608031A0B08DD96D4DD0510...0571756572790A08757365725F303031
2018-10-03 18:33:01.254 UTC [msp/identity] Sign -> DEBU 006 Sign: digest: EC2BC9E95F782423D60A74DBBF49D71F85E79E8EEB6DD16EFD306EEF0F6B9536
Query Result: {"id":"user_001","firstName":"John","lastName":"Smith","ssn":"9999","policyNumber":"4394497111/1"}
```

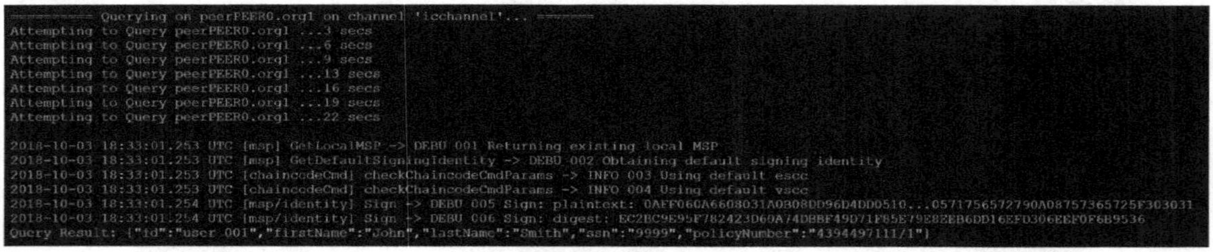

Insuree added in our block chain

Invoking add broker

Let's onboard a broker to our insurance claim blockchain, as follows:

```
peer chaincode invoke -o orderer.ic.com:7050 -C icchannel -n iccc -c
'{"Args":["AddCompany","broker_001","BROKER","BNC Brokerage"]}'
```

Here is the result:

Onboarding a broker to our insurance claim blockchain

Invoking add insurer

Add the last party insurer to the insurance claim blockchain, as follows:

```
peer chaincode invoke -o orderer.ic.com:7050 -C icchannel -n iccc -c
'{"Args":["AddCompany","insurer_001","INSURER","Western Insurance"]}'
```

The output that's displayed is as follows:

Adding a last party insurer to insurance claim blockchain

Invoking ReportLost

All of the participants have joined the network, and it is time to start the insurance claim process. An insuree reports a claim to a broker, Here is the command to invoke 'ReportLost' chaincode.

```
peer chaincode invoke -o orderer.ic.com:7050 -C icchannel -n iccc -c
'{"Args":["ReportLost","claim_001", "I was in Destiny shopping center and
lost my IPhone 8", "user_001", "broker_001"]}
```

The following output will be displayed:

Isuree reporting a claim to a broker

Invoking RequestedInfo

A broker provides the requested information, as follows:

```
peer chaincode invoke -o orderer.ic.com:7050 -C icchannel -n iccc -c
'{"Args":["RequestedInfo","claim_001", "Broker processsed user John Smith
report and sent Requested Info to user.", "insurer_001"]}'
```

The following output will be displayed:

Providing the requested information

Invoking SubmitClaim

A broker submits a claim to an issuer, as follows:

```
peer chaincode invoke -o orderer.ic.com:7050 -C icchannel -n iccc -c
'{"Args":["SubmitClaim","claim_001", "Broker submitted a claim"]}'
```

The following output will be displayed:

Submitting a claim to the issuer

Invoking ConfirmClaimSubmission

An issuer confirms the claim, as follows:

```
peer chaincode invoke -o orderer.ic.com:7050 -C icchannel -n iccc -c
'{"Args":["ConfirmClaimSubmission","claim_001", "Insurer received and
confirmed a claim"]}'
```

The following output will be displayed:

Confirming the claim

Invoking ApproveClaim

An issuer processes and approves a claim, as follows:

```
peer chaincode invoke -o orderer.ic.com:7050 -C icchannel -n iccc -c
'{"Args":["ApproveClaim","claim_001", "Insurer processed and approved the
claim."]}'
```

The following output will be displayed:

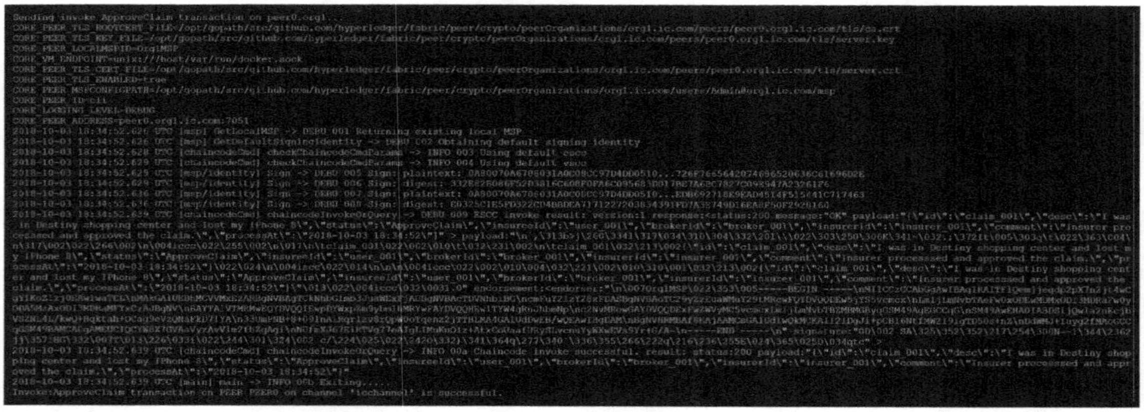

Processing and approving the claim

Querying claim history

After an issuer approves the claim, the entire process flow is done and we can use the Fabric API to query the entire life cycle of the claim, as follows:

```
peer chaincode query -C icchannel -n iccc -c
'{"Args":["getHistory","claim_001"]}'
```

From the output obtained from this query, we can see the entire Fabric transaction history of the claim request.

This ends our test execution.

End-to-end test execution

We have gone over each step of insurance claim fabric execution. To simplify the entire end-to-end application flow, you can navigate to the `insurance-claim` folder and then run the following command:

```
cd ~/insurance-claim
#change path if insurance-claim directory is different
export PATH=/home/ubuntu/insurance-claim/bin:$PATH
./icn.sh -m up
```

The output result will be as follows:

```
ubuntu@ip-172-31-14-103:~/insurance-claim$ ./icn.sh -m up
/home/ubuntu/insurance-claim/bin/cryptogen

##########################################################
##### Generate certificates using cryptogen tool #########
##########################################################

org1.ic.com
org2.ic.com
org3.ic.com

/home/ubuntu/insurance-claim/bin/configtxgen
##########################################################
#########  Generating Orderer Genesis block ##############
##########################################################
2018-12-12 18:23:25.419 UTC [common/configtx/tool] main -> INFO 001 Loading configuration
2018-12-12 18:23:25.453 UTC [common/configtx/tool] doOutputBlock -> INFO 002 Generating genesis block
2018-12-12 18:23:25.455 UTC [common/configtx/tool] doOutputBlock -> INFO 003 Writing genesis block

#################################################################
### Generating channel configuration transaction 'channel.tx' ###
#################################################################
2018-12-12 18:23:25.481 UTC [common/configtx/tool] main -> INFO 001 Loading configuration
2018-12-12 18:23:25.484 UTC [common/configtx/tool] doOutputChannelCreateTx -> INFO 002 Generating new channel configtx
2018-12-12 18:23:25.484 UTC [common/configtx/tool] doOutputChannelCreateTx -> INFO 003 Writing new channel tx

#################################################################
### Generating an configuration transaction 'Org1MSPanchors.tx' ###
#################################################################
2018-12-12 18:23:25.505 UTC [common/configtx/tool] main -> INFO 001 Loading configuration
```

Simplifying the entire end to end application flow

The final output is as follows:

```
CORE_VM_ENDPOINT=unix:///host/var/run/docker.sock
CORE_PEER_TLS_CERT_FILE=/opt/gopath/src/github.com/hyperledger/fabric/peer/crypto/peerOrganizations/org1.ic.com/peers/peer0
.org1.ic.com/tls/server.crt
CORE_PEER_TLS_ENABLED=true
CORE_PEER_MSPCONFIGPATH=/opt/gopath/src/github.com/hyperledger/fabric/peer/crypto/peerOrganizations/org1.ic.com/users/Admin
@org1.ic.com/msp
CORE_PEER_ID=cli
CORE_LOGGING_LEVEL=DEBUG
CORE_PEER_ADDRESS=peer0.org1.ic.com:7051
========= History Querying on peerPEER0.org1 on channel 'icchannel'... =======
Attempting to Query peerPEER0.org1 ...3 secs
Attempting to Query peerPEER0.org1 ...6 secs
Attempting to Query peerPEER0.org1 ...9 secs
Attempting to Query peerPEER0.org1 ...12 secs
Attempting to Query peerPEER0.org1 ...15 secs
Attempting to Query peerPEER0.org1 ...18 secs
Attempting to Query peerPEER0.org1 ...21 secs

2018-12-12 18:27:48.570 UTC [main] InitCmd -> WARN 001 CORE_LOGGING_LEVEL is no longer supported, please use the FABRIC_LOG
GING_SPEC environment variable
2018-12-12 18:27:48.586 UTC [main] SetOrdererEnv -> WARN 002 CORE_LOGGING_LEVEL is no longer supported, please use the FABR
IC_LOGGING_SPEC environment variable
[{"txId":"e9febd16b271af72b4cbade2f26118fa390945cda2bc0127be84c82dc3ab2793","value":{"id":"claim_001","desc":"I was in Dest
iny shopping center and lost my IPhone 8","status":"ReportLost","insureeId":"user_001","brokerId":"broker_001","insurerId":
"","comment":"","processAt":"2018-12-12 18:25:39"}},{"txId":"2c4797d86995dd9a3fb02221bbe2cf016aee05f2c3d5f33637fd823f4cef3c
92","value":{"id":"claim_001","desc":"I was in Destiny shopping center and lost my IPhone 8","status":"RequestedInfo","insu
reeId":"user_001","brokerId":"broker_001","insurerId":"insurer_001","comment":"Broker processsed user John Smith report and
 sent Requested Info to user.","processAt":"2018-12-12 18:26:01"}},{"txId":"6535cef807479568141e4622f13bb439941b69fa1dc21c5
5f05c55119aca9b0b","value":{"id":"claim_001","desc":"I was in Destiny shopping center and lost my IPhone 8","status":"Submi
tClaim","insureeId":"user_001","brokerId":"broker_001","insurerId":"insurer_001","comment":"Broker submitted a claim","proc
essAt":"2018-12-12 18:26:22"}},{"txId":"1ce6504a6c8b72f71334100e5092e7579fc5486990810e77fe4b658faf837d14","value":{"id":"cl
aim_001","desc":"I was in Destiny shopping center and lost my IPhone 8","status":"ConfirmClaimSubmission","insureeId":"user
_001","brokerId":"broker_001","insurerId":"insurer_001","comment":"Insurer received and confirmed a claim","processAt":"201
8-12-12 18:26:44"}},{"txId":"e57d089c7033380148e85a15bb156fc8f824d0bb983769af8023ab2bba664336","value":{"id":"claim_001","d
esc":"I was in Destiny shopping center and lost my IPhone 8","status":"ApproveClaim","insureeId":"user_001","brokerId":"bro
ker_001","insurerId":"insurer_001","comment":"Insurer processsed and approved the claim.","processAt":"2018-12-12 18:27:05"
}}]

======== Insuance Claim End to End Test Completed ==========
```

Insurance claim End to End Test completes

Summary

In this chapter, we have learned about the basics of Hyperledger Fabric's. After setting up a development environment, we wrote a chaincode for an insurance claim use case. We then studied fabric composer configuration. Finally, we ran the end-to-end fabric test execution for our insurance claim application. We can see that it is quite complex to use Hyperledger Fabric to implement an insurance claim application. In the next chapter, we will learn how to use Hyperledger Composer to quickly write an insurance claim application.

6 Implementing Business Networks Using Hyperledger Composer

Hyperledger Composer is a high-level toolset and framework that was made to quickly build and run applications on top of a Hyperledger Fabric blockchain.

We learned about Hyperledger Fabric in the previous chapter, so you already know that developing a Fabric-based application is quite complex as it needs to handle many configurations at the network level.

In this chapter, we will discuss the following topics:

- Hyperledger Composer—a quick overview
- Setting up a Hyperledger Composer environment
- Analyzing business scenarios
- The business network archive
- Implementing business transaction functions

Hyperledger Composer – a quick overview

Hyperledger Composer is a set of JavaScript-based high-level toolsets and frameworks that simplify and quickly build and run an application on top of a Hyperledger Fabric blockchain. Business owners and developers can quickly create smart contracts and applications via the composer tool. The composer tool generates a RESTful endpoint to interact with fabric channels. Instead of writing chaincode using Golang, Composer uses model language to generate a business network archive (`.BNA`) file for the blockchain network.

Here is an example of a Hyperledger Composer solution architecture:

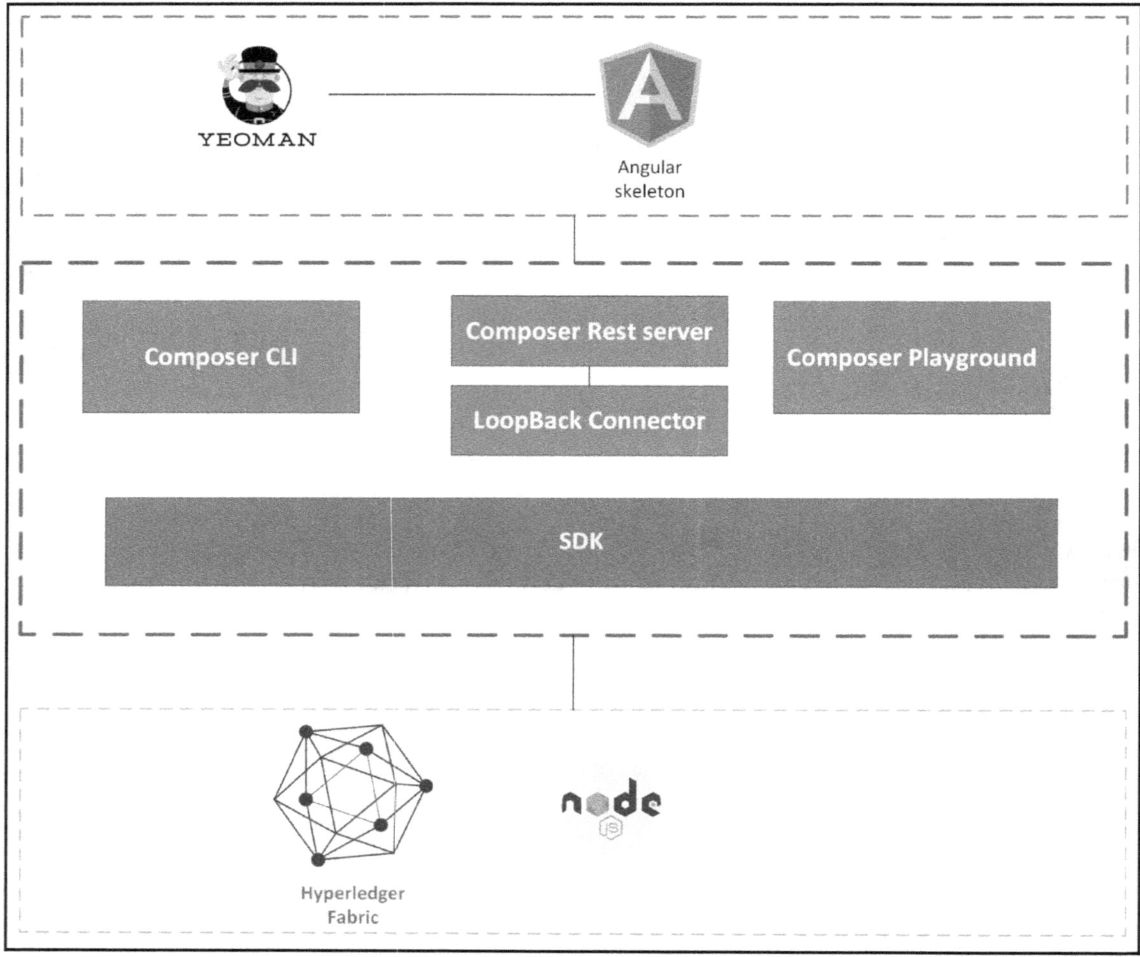

Hyperledger Composer contains the components that are listed in the following sections.

Yeoman generator

The npm module generator-hyperledger-composer in Yeoman is used to make templates for Hyperledger Composer. It supports and generates three different types of templates:

- CLI application
- Angular 2 application
- Skeleton business network

You can use Yeoman's generated angular skeleton to connect to the Hyperledger Composer REST server.

Composer REST server

Composer's REST server utilizes a standalone Node.js process and exposes a set of RESTful API endpoints from a deployed composer business network. These generated APIs can interact with fabric chaincode. The side code can then trigger **create**, **read**, **update**, **delete** (**CRUD**) for assets, participants, and transactions.

LoopBack connector

The LoopBack connector utilises the Node.js LoopBack framework to expose GET/POST/PUT/DELETE operations for the assets, participants, and transactions defined in the business network.

JavaScript SDK

The JavaScript SDK API is used to interact with the deployed business network. It is comprised of the client and admin APIs.

The client APIs provide query, create, update, and delete resources (asset and participant), and submit transactions from client applications.

The admin API is used to deploy the business network.

Composer playground

The Hyperledger Composer playground is a browser-based interface to create and test business networks. You can use the playground to build and test your business network.

Composer-cli

Composer-cli is a command-line tool that lets you deploy and manage business networks.

Here is a list of some commands:

Command	**Description**
`composer archive create`	Command to create a business network archive file (`nba`).
`composer archive list`	Verifies the contents of a business network archive.
`composer card create`	Creates a business network card from individual components.
`composer card delete`	Deletes a business network card from individual components.
`composer card list`	Lists all business network cards stored in the local wallet.
`composer network deploy`	Deploys a business network archive from local disk to a Hyperledger Fabric network.
`composer network list`	Lists the details of the business network card.
`composer network ping`	Tests the connection to a deployed business network.

Setting up a Hyperledger Composer environment

We just reviewed the Hyperledger Composer solution architecture. In this section, we will set up the Hyperledger development environment.

Installation prerequisites

Before we install the composer tools, make sure you have the required prerequisites by following the *Setup of Hyperledger Fabric environment—installing prerequisites* section.

Installing the development environment

The following are the installation commands for developing the environment:

- Installing the CLI tools:

```
npm install -g composer-cli@0.20
```

- Installing `composer-rest-server`:

```
npm install -g composer-rest-server@0.20
```

- Installing Hyperledger Composer generator:

```
npm install -g generator-hyperledger-composer@0.20
```

- Installing Yeoman:

```
npm install -g yo
```

- Installing playground:

```
npm install -g composer-playground
```

- Installing fabric runtime:

  Download and install fabric runtime for the composer as follows:

```
mkdir ~/fabric-devserver && cd ~/fabric-devserver
curl -O https://raw.githubusercontent.com/hyperledger/composer-
tools/master/packages/fabric-dev-servers/fabric-dev-servers.zip
unzip fabric-dev-servers.zip
export FABRIC_VERSION=hlfv12
./downloadFabric.sh
```

At this step, you have installed everything required for the typical composer development environment.

Analyzing business scenarios

In `Chapter 5`, *Exploring an Enterprise Blockchain Application Using Hyperledger Fabric,* we discussed the blockchain use case for the insurance claim. It includes the following steps:

1. An insuree reports a claim to a broker
2. A broker provides requested information

3. A broker submits a claim to an issuer
4. An issuer confirms the claim
5. An issuer processes and approves the claim

In this chapter, we will use the same insurance claim use case, but also build the end-to-end application via Hyperledger Composer.

Business network archive

Composer business is comprised of four different types of files: model file (`.cto`), script file (`.js`), access control list (ACL) file (`.acl`), and query file (`.qry`).

Network model file (.cto)

A CTO file is composed of the following elements:

Element	Description
A single namespace	Defines the composer model namespace; every `.cto` model file requires a namespace.
Resources - asset	Anything of value that can be exchanged between parties.
Resources - participant	Business network member.
Resources - enum	A data type consisting of a set of named values.
Resources - concept	Any object you want to model that is not one of the other types.
Resources - transactions	Defines the blockchain business logic.
Resources - events	Blockchain transaction notification.
Import	Imports resources from other namespaces.

The composer model language, like other programming languages, has data types including String, Double, Integer, and so on.

Let's see some samples of assets, participants, transactions, and events.

IBM Bluemix provides a browser version playground without installation; we can use this tool to do a quick prototype. Here is the link: `https://composer-playground.mybluemix.net/`.

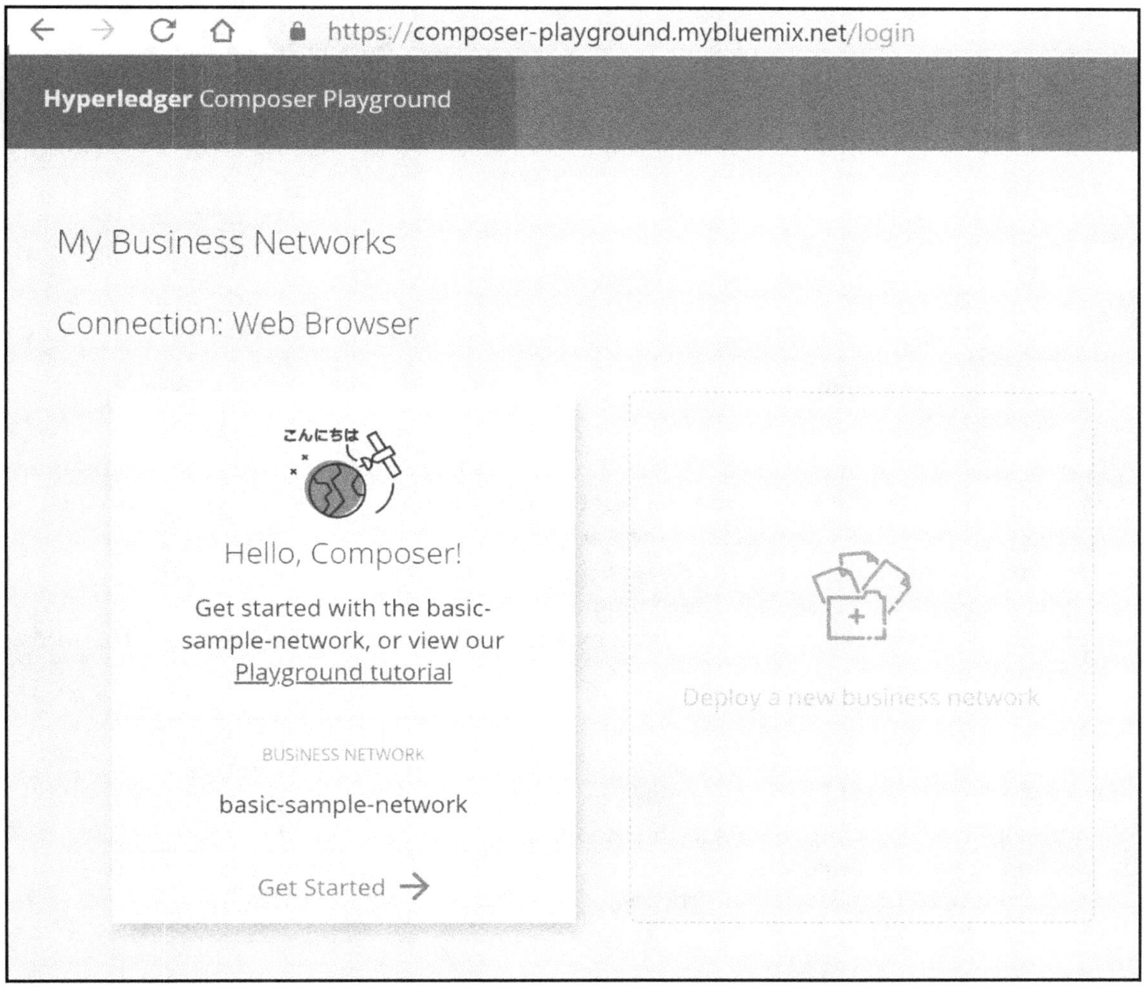

Connect to **basic-sample-network**. Playground will generate some default sample assets, participants, transactions, and events for you, for example:

```
sample.cto
/**
* Sample business network definition.
 */
namespace org.example.basic
asset SampleAsset identified by assetId {
  o String assetId
  --> SampleParticipant owner
  o String value
```

```
}
participant SampleParticipant identified by participantId {
  o String participantId
  o String firstName
  o String lastName
}
transaction SampleTransaction {
  --> SampleAsset asset
  o String newValue
}
event SampleEvent {
  --> SampleAsset asset
  o String oldValue
  o String newValue
}
```

A `namespace org.example.basic` was defined in `sample.cto.SampleAsset` and is an example of an `Asset` class. It defines an asset whose name is followed by an identifying `field.o String assetId`: a field of the `SampleAsset.--> SampleParticipant owner`: field point to `SampleParticipant instance.SampleParticipant` is an example of a `Participant` class, the syntax is similar to `SampleAsset.SampleTransaction` is an example of a transaction `class.SampleEvent` is an example of an event class.

Script file (.js)

We define transactions and events in the model file, a script file that implements these transaction functions. Decorators within *comments* are used to annotate the functions with metadata required for transaction processing, for example:

```
/**
 * Sample transaction processor function.
 * @param {org.example.basic.SampleTransaction} tx The sample transaction
instance.
 * @transaction
 */
async function sampleTransaction(tx) {  // eslint-disable-line no-unused-
vars
..
    emit(event);
}
```

In the `sampleTransaction` function, the `@param` tag is followed by the resource name of the transaction that triggers the transaction processor function. `@transaction` marks this function as a transaction processor function.

Access control list (ACL) file (.acl)

An ACL file defines the permission of the participants in the business network, for example:

```
rule OwnerHasFullAccessToTheirAssets {
    description: "Allow all participants full access to their assets"
    participant(p): "org.example.basic.SampleParticipant"
    operation: ALL
    resource(r): "org.example.basic.SampleAsset"
    condition: (r.owner.getIdentifier() === p.getIdentifier())
    action: ALLOW
}
```

In the preceding ACL example, it specifies that the participant is `SampleParticipant`. Any instance registered as `SampleParticipant` can perform `ALL` operations on all instances of `org.example.SampleAsset`. This transaction is triggered when the `SampleAsset` owner is the same as the participant who submitted a transaction.

Query file (.qry)

A query file defines the queries that are used to return data about the blockchain world state. The query syntax is quite similar to SQL language, for example:

```
query queryName {
    description: "Select SampleAsset by assetId "
    statement:
        SELECT org.example.basic.SampleAsset
            WHERE (_$assetId = assetId)
}
```

Designing business models

Now that we have reviewed the basic composer model language and structure, it is time to implement an insurance claim using Hyperledger Composer.

For simplicity's sake, we will allow participants to have permission to read and write for all resources in this example. Remove the sample resource related to ACL and update the rule as follows:

```
rule EverybodyCanReadEverything {
    description: "Allow all participants read access to all resources"
    participant: "**"
    operation: READ
    resource: "com.packt.quickstart.claim.*"
    action: ALLOW
}
rule EverybodyCanSubmitTransactions {
    description: "Allow all participants to submit transactions"
    participant: "**"
    operation: CREATE
    resource: "**"
    action: ALLOW
}
```

With simplified ACL, we start to work on our model file as follows:

1. Rename `sample.cto` as `insurance-claim.cto`
2. Change namespace to `com.packt.quickstart.claim` and remove the remaining code
3. Define the participants and assets

   We wrote a chaincode called `claimcontract.go` in `Chapter 5`, *Exploring an Enterprise Blockchain Application using Hyperledger Fabric,* that defines a struct for insuree, broker insurer, and claim. We can define participants and assets similar to this struct. It is quite straightforward, as follows:

```
namespace com.packt.quickstart.claim
participant Insuree identified by id {
  o String id
  o String firstName
  o String lastName
  o String ssn
  o String policyNumber
}
participant Company identified by id {
  o String id
  o String type
  o String name
}
asset Claim identified by id {
  o String id
```

```
    o String desc
    o Integer status
    o String insureeId
    o String brokerId
    o String insurerId
    o String comment
    o String processAt
  }
```

4. Define the transactions and events. By using the `Init` function, we onboard insuree, as follows:

```
transaction Init {
  o String insureeId
  o String firstName
  o String lastName
  o String ssn
  o String policyNumber
}
event InitEvent {
  --> Insuree insuree
}
```

5. Composer's JavaScript API provides CRUD to create resources, including the participant. For the insurer and broker, we will use this approach. We will explain this in more detail when we do testing.
6. Define `ReportLost`: An insuree reports a claim to a broker—this starts a claim, as follows:

```
transaction ReportLost {
  o String claimId
  o String desc
  o String insureeId
  o String brokerId
}
event ReportLostEvent {
   --> Claim claim
}
```

7. Define `RequestedInfo`: A broker provides the requested information, as follows:

```
transaction RequestedInfo {
  --> Claim claim
}
event RequestedInfoEvent {
  --> Claim claim
}
```

8. Define `SubmitClaim`: A broker submits a claim to an issuer.
9. Define `ConfirmClaimSubmission`: An issuer confirms the claim.
10. Define `ApproveClaim`: An issuer process and approves the claim.

Step 8, 9, and 10 are transaction functions, and are very similar to step 7.

We have defined all of our transactions, participants, and assets in the model file. As a next step, we will implement the transaction we defined in the model file.

Implementing the business transaction function

We learned how to implement a transaction function in the previous section by reviewing `SampleTransaction`. Following a similar approach, we will implement an insurance claim transaction function. Rename `sample.js` to `logic.js`.

Implement the `Init` function, as follows:

```
Init() function is used to register insuree person information.
/**
  * Create the insuree
  * @param {com.packt.quickstart.claim.Init} initalAppliation - the
InitialApplication transaction
  * @transaction
  */
 async function Init(application) { // eslint-disable-line no-unused-vars
     const factory = getFactory();
     const namespace = 'com.packt.quickstart.claim';
     const insuree = factory.newResource(namespace, 'Insuree',
application.insureeId);
     insuree.firstName = application.firstName;;     insuree.lastName =
application.lastName
```

```
        insuree.ssn = application.ssn;;
        insuree.policyNumber = application.policyNumber;;
        const participantRegistry = await
getParticipantRegistry(insuree.getFullyQualifiedType());
        await participantRegistry.add(insuree);
        // emit event
        const initEventEvent = factory.newEvent(namespace, 'InitEvent');
        initEventEvent.insuree = insuree;
        emit(initEventEvent);
    }
```

Implement ReportLost and, set up and create a claim, as follows:

```
/**
  * insuree report lost item
  * @param {com.packt.quickstart.claim.ReportLost} ReportLost - the
ReportLost transaction
  * @transaction
  */
 async function ReportLost(request) {
        const factory = getFactory();
        const namespace = 'com.packt.quickstart.claim';
        let claimId = request.claimId;
        let desc = request.desc;
        let insureeId = request.insureeId;
        let brokerId = request.brokerId;
        const claim = factory.newResource(namespace, 'Claim', claimId);
        claim.desc = desc;
        claim.status = "ReportLost";
        claim.insureeId = insureeId;
        claim.brokerId = brokerId;
        claim.insurerId = "";
        claim.comment = "";
        claim.processAt = (new Date()).toString();
        const claimRegistry = await
getAssetRegistry(claim.getFullyQualifiedType());
        await claimRegistry.add(claim);
        // emit event
        const reportLostEvent = factory.newEvent(namespace,
'ReportLostEvent');
        reportLostEvent.claim = claim;
        emit(reportLostEvent); }
```

Implement `RequestedInfo` to verify and update the claim status, as follows:

```
/**
  * broker send Requested Info to insuree
  * @param {com.packt.quickstart.claim.RequestedInfo} RequestedInfo - the
RequestedInfo transaction
  * @transaction
  */
 async function RequestedInfo(request) { // eslint-disable-line no-unused-
vars
     const factory = getFactory();
     const namespace = 'com.packt.quickstart.claim';
     let claim = request.claim;
     if (claim.status !== 'ReportLost') {
         throw new Error ('This claim should be in ReportLost status');
     }
     claim.status = 'RequestedInfo';
     claim.processAt = (new Date()).toString();
     const assetRegistry = await
getAssetRegistry(request.claim.getFullyQualifiedType());
     await assetRegistry.update(claim);
     // emit event
     const requestedInfoEventEvent = factory.newEvent(namespace,
'RequestedInfoEvent');
     requestedInfoEventEvent.claim = claim;
     emit(requestedInfoEventEvent); }
```

Implement `SubmitClaim`, `ConfirmClaimSubmission`, and `ApproveClaim`. These functions are similar to `RequestedInfo`.

Testing in the playground

We just implemented all model and logic files in the previous section, so it is time to test our composer application:

1. Click on the **Deploy changes** button on the left bottom panel of the playground. This will deploy the composer code.
2. Click **Test** link on the top navigation bar. It will pop up the submit transaction page. Select the init method from the transaction type drop down. Enter the JSON value, as shown in the following screenshot; the input data is the same as what we tested in `Chapter 5`, *Exploring an Enterprise Blockchain Application using Hyperledger Fabric*. Instantiate the fabric chaincode step. Submit the transaction, as follows:

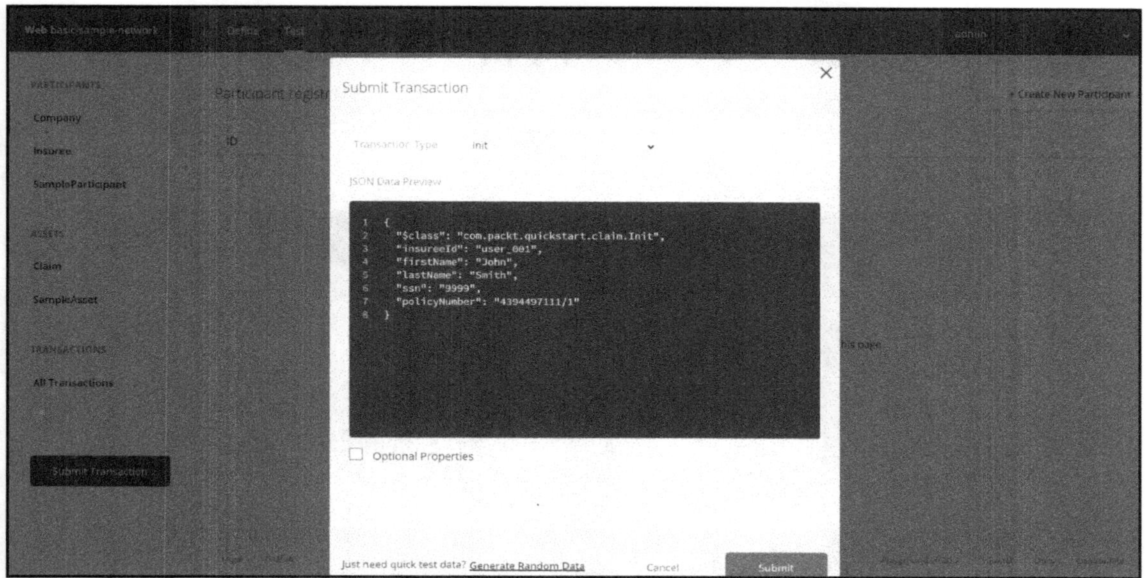

If transaction submission is successful, we will be able to see that the insuree participant has been created, for example:

Web basic-sample-network   Define   Test

PARTICIPANTS

Company

Insuree

SampleParticipant

ASSETS

Claim

SampleAsset

TRANSACTIONS

All Transactions

Participant registry for com.packt.quickstart.claim.Insuree

ID	Data
user_001	{ "$class": "com.packt.quickstart.claim.Insuree", "id": "user_001", "firstName": "John", "lastName": "Smith", "ssn": "9999", "policyNumber": "4394497111/1" }

Collapse

3. Now, let's onboard the broker and insurer. Click company in the participant section and click **Create New Participant**. Enter the broker data in, the same way that we did it for the `chaincodeInvokeAddBroker` step in `Chapter 5`, *Exploring an Enterprise Blockchain Application using Hyperledger Fabric*. Click **Create New,** as follows:

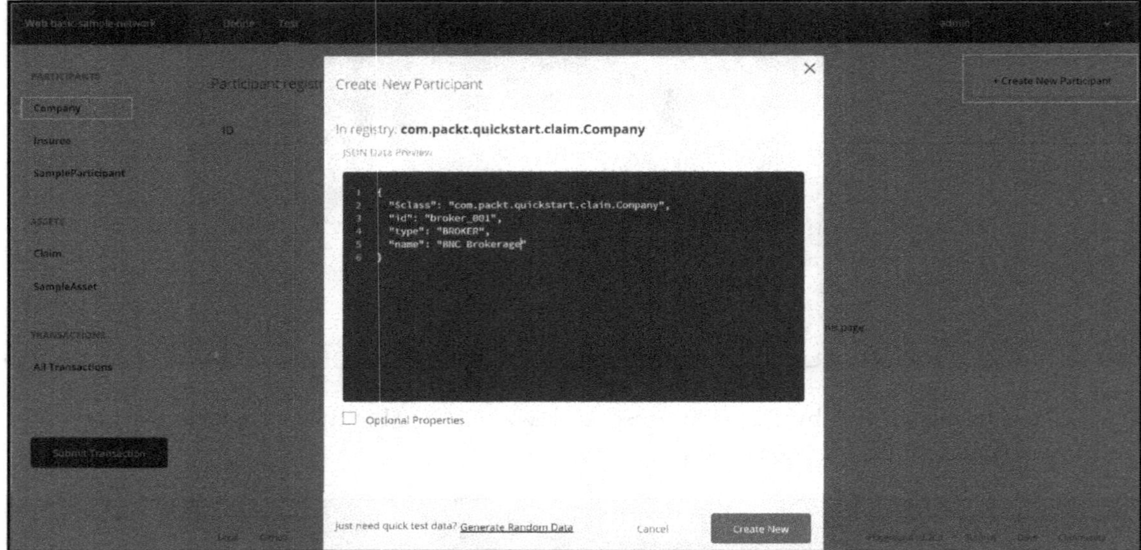

If the transaction submission succeeds, this will onboard the broker. Repeat this same step to onboard the insurer, as follows:

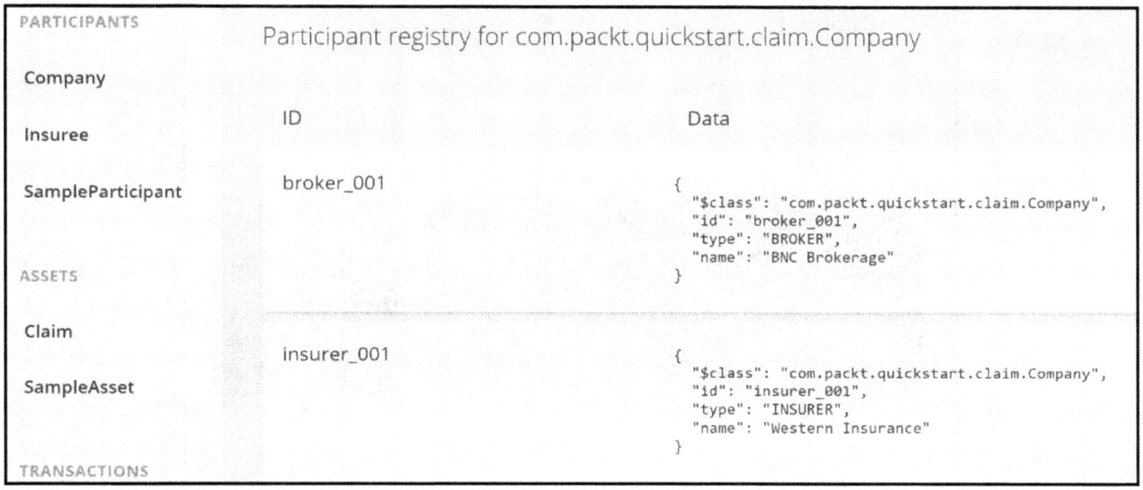

PARTICIPANTS

Company

Insuree

SampleParticipant

ASSETS

Claim

SampleAsset

TRANSACTIONS

Participant registry for com.packt.quickstart.claim.Company

ID	Data
broker_001	{ "$class": "com.packt.quickstart.claim.Company", "id": "broker_001", "type": "BROKER", "name": "BNC Brokerage" }
insurer_001	{ "$class": "com.packt.quickstart.claim.Company", "id": "insurer_001", "type": "INSURER", "name": "Western Insurance" }

4. Submit `ReportLost`, as follows:

Here is the result:

Asset registry for com.packt.quickstart.claim.Claim

ID	Data
claim_001	

```
{
  "$class": "com.packt.quickstart.claim.Claim",
  "id": "claim_001",
  "desc": "I was in Destiny shopping center and lost my IPhone 8",
  "status": "ReportLost",
  "insureeId": "user_001",
  "brokerId": "broker_001",
  "insurerId": "",
  "comment": "",
  "processAt": "Sat Oct 06 2018 03:18:42 GMT-0400 (Eastern Daylight Time)"
}
```

Collapse

5. Test `RequestedInfo` with the following result:

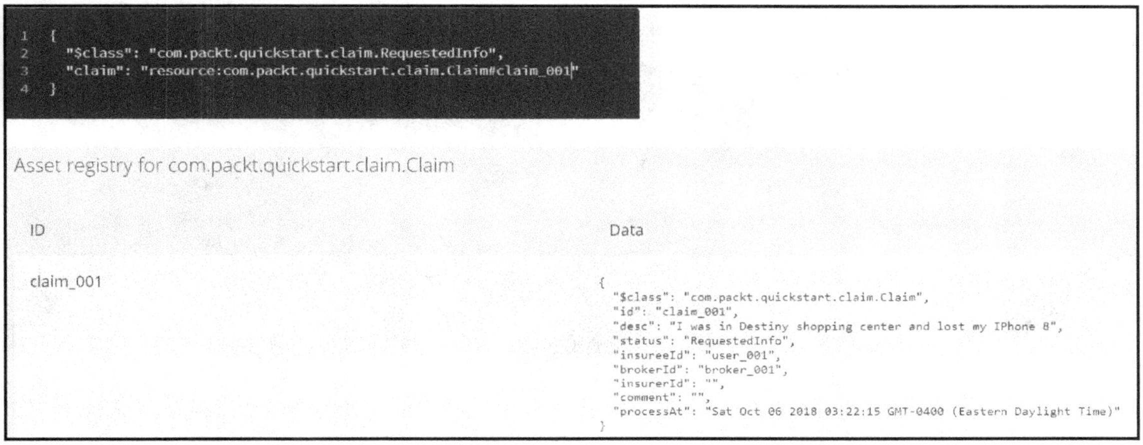

```
{
  "$class": "com.packt.quickstart.claim.RequestedInfo",
  "claim": "resource:com.packt.quickstart.claim.Claim#claim_001"
}
```

Asset registry for com.packt.quickstart.claim.Claim

ID	Data
claim_001	{ "$class": "com.packt.quickstart.claim.Claim", "id": "claim_001", "desc": "I was in Destiny shopping center and lost my IPhone 8", "status": "RequestedInfo", "insureeId": "user_001", "brokerId": "broker_001", "insurerId": "", "comment": "", "processAt": "Sat Oct 06 2018 03:22:15 GMT-0400 (Eastern Daylight Time)" }

The remaining steps (`SubmitClaim`, `ConfirmClaimSubmission`, and `ApproveClaim`) are very similar to `RequestedInfo`.

Deploying a business network

We have tested the composer application in the playground, so next we will deploy it to the blockchain:

1. Create a folder called `insurance-claim-network`, and navigate to the folder.
2. Generate a business network project template, as follows:

```
yo hyperledger-composer:businessnetwork
```

It will prompt a few questions. Enter `insurance-claim-network` as the network name and choose the empty template network, as shown in the following screenshot:

```
Welcome to the business network generator
? Business network name: insurance-claim-network
? Description: create insurance claim
? Author name:  brian wu
? Author email: brian.wu@smartchart.tech
? License: Apache-2.0
? Namespace: com.packt.quickstart.claim
? Do you want to generate an empty template network? Yes: generate an empty template network
   create package.json
   create README.md
   create models/com.packt.quickstart.claim.cto
   create permissions.acl
   create .eslintrc.yml
```

This will generate a few files with a default template. Replace the contents of `com.packt.quickstart`
`.claim.cto` with our earlier tested model file.

Create a new folder called `lib`, under the `lib` folder, and copy the tested `logic.js` in here.
Replace `permissions.acl` with the tested `acl` file, as follows:

```
.
├── lib
│   └── logic.js
├── models
│   └── com.packt.quickstart.claim.cto
├── package.json
├── permissions.acl
└── README.md
```

3. Start Hyperledger Fabric, as follows:

```
cd ~/fabric-devservers
    export FABRIC_VERSION=hlfv12
    ./startFabric.sh
    ./createPeerAdminCard.sh
```

This will create `PeerAdminCard`, as shown in the following screenshot:

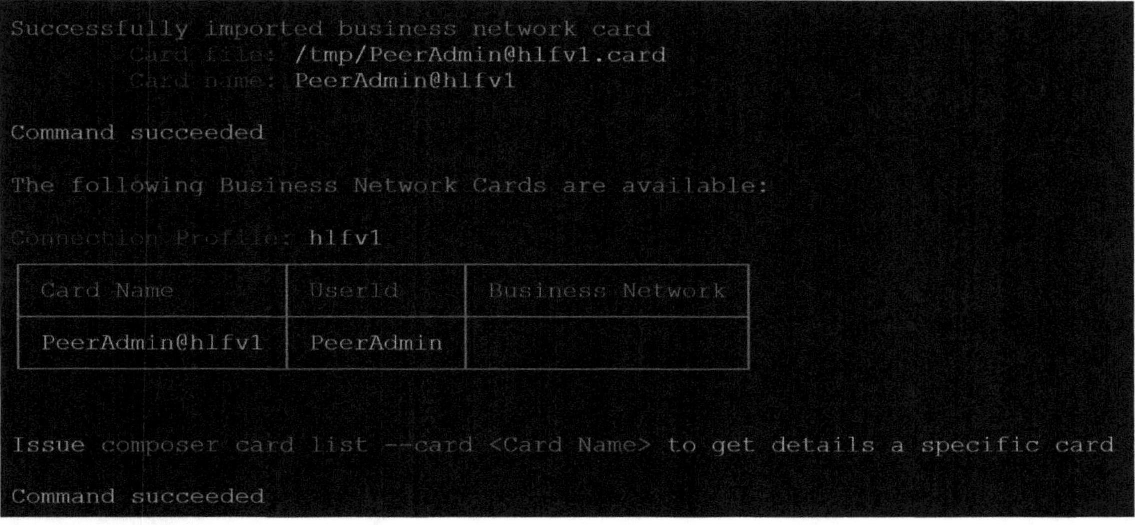

Successfully imported business network card
Card file: /tmp/PeerAdmin@hlfv1.card
Card name: PeerAdmin@hlfv1
Command succeeded
The following Business Network Cards are available:
Connection Profile: hlfv1
Card Name
UserId
Business Network
PeerAdmin@hlfv1
PeerAdmin
Issue composer card list --card <Card Name> to get details a specific card
Command succeeded

4. Generate a business network archive. From the `insurance-claim-network` directory, run the following command:

```
composer archive create -t dir -n
```

This will generate `insurance-claim-network@0.0.1.bna`.

5. Install the business network. From the `insurance-claim-network` directory, run the following command:

```
composer network install --card PeerAdmin@hlfv1 --archiveFile
insurance-claim-network@0.0.1.bna
```

6. Start the business network. From the `insurance-claim-network` directory, run the following command:

```
composer network start --networkName insurance-claim-network --
networkVersion 0.0.1 --networkAdmin admin --networkAdminEnrollSecret
adminpw --card PeerAdmin@hlfv1 --file networkadmin.card
```

7. Import the network admin card. From the `insurance-claim-network` in directory, run the following command. This will import `insurance-claim-network` to the network:

   ```
   composer card import --file networkadmin.card
   ```

8. Check if the business network has been deployed successfully. From the `insurance-claim-network` directory, run the following command:

   ```
   composer network ping --card admin@insurance-claim-network
   ```

   The result should look as follows:

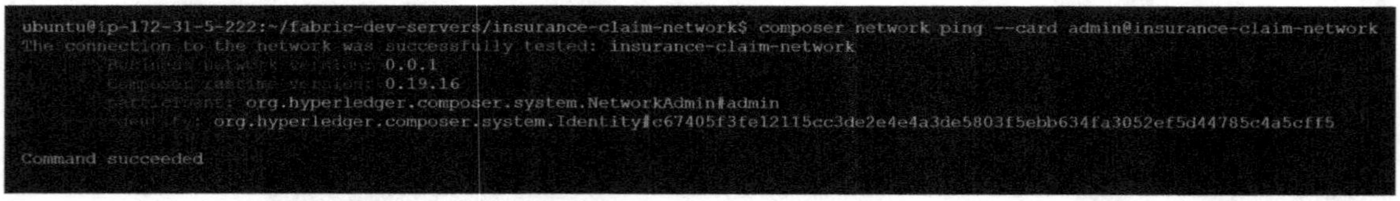

```
ubuntu@ip-172-31-5-222:~/fabric-dev-servers/insurance-claim-network$ composer network ping --card admin@insurance-claim-network
The connection to the network was successfully tested: insurance-claim-network
        0.0.1
        0.19.16
        org.hyperledger.composer.system.NetworkAdmin#admin
        org.hyperledger.composer.system.Identity#c67405f3fe12115cc3de2e4e4a3de5803f5ebb634fa3052ef5d44785c4a5cff5

Command succeeded
```

Checking if the business network been deployed successfully

Integrating with REST server

We just deployed `insurance-claim-network` in the fabric network. The next step is to build an insurance-claim client API to interact with the smart contract function in the network. The Hyperledger Composer REST server can be used to generate a REST API. A REST client can call these end point functions and interact with the business network chaincode from the Fabric blockchain.

Generating the Hyperledger Composer REST API

Run the following command to generate a composer server API:

```
composer-rest-server
```

Enter `admin@insurance-claim-network` from the business network card, as shown in the following screenshot:

```
ubuntu@ip-172-31-5-222:~/fabric-dev-servers/insurance-claim-network$ composer-rest-server
? Enter the name of the business network card to use: admin@insurance-claim-network
? Specify if you want namespaces in the generated REST API: never use namespaces
? Specify if you want to use an API key to secure the REST API: No
? Specify if you want to enable authentication for the REST API using Passport: No
? Specify if you want to enable the explorer test interface: Yes
? Specify a key if you want to enable dynamic logging:
? Specify if you want to enable event publication over WebSockets: Yes
? Specify if you want to enable TLS security for the REST API: No

To restart the REST server using the same options, issue the following command:
   composer-rest-server -c admin@insurance-claim-network -n never -u true -w true

Discovering types from business network definition ...
Discovering the Returning Transactions..
Discovered types from business network definition
Generating schemas for all types in business network definition ...
Generated schemas for all types in business network definition
Adding schemas for all types to Loopback ...
Added schemas for all types to Loopback
Web server listening at: http://localhost:3000
Browse your REST API at http://localhost:3000/explorer
```

Entering business network card

This will a generate the REST API and expose it as `http://serverIP:3000` and `http://serverIP:3000/explorer`.

Open the explore URL. You will see the generated REST endpoints, as follows:

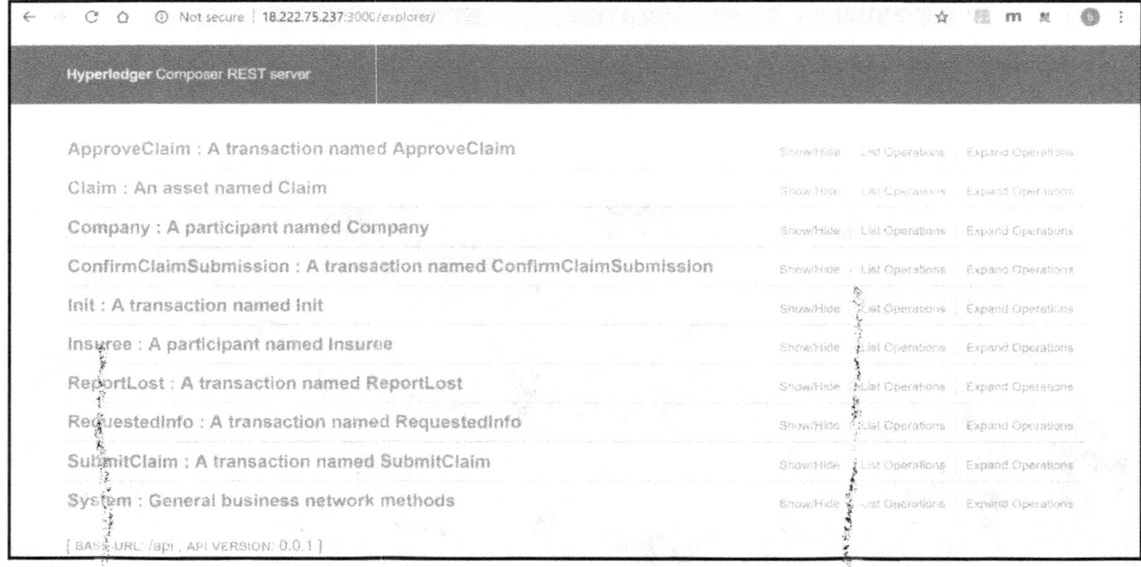

Let's try a number of methods to demonstrate how these endpoints interact with the fabric network.

Select the `init Post` method from endpoints, provide the post JSON data, and click the Try it out! button. The example of JSON data is shown as follows:

```
{
  "$class": "com.packt.quickstart.claim.Init",
  "insureeId": "user-001",
  "firstName": "John",
  "lastName": "Smith",
  "ssn": "9999",
  "policyNumber": "string"
}
```

Here is a screenshot that shows the result after clicking the **Try it out!** button:

Try it out! Hide Response

Curl

```
curl -X POST --header 'Content-Type: application/json' --header 'Accept: application/json' -d '{ \
   "$class": "com.packt.quickstart.claim.Company", \
   "id": "insurer_001", \
   "type": "INSURER", \
   "name": "Western Insurance" \
 }' 'http://18.222.75.237:3000/api/Company'
```

Request URL

```
http://18.222.75.237:3000/api/Company
```

Response Body

```
{
  "$class": "com.packt.quickstart.claim.Company",
  "id": "insurer_001",
  "type": "INSURER",
  "name": "Western Insurance"
}
```

Response Code

```
200
```

Response Headers

```
{
  "date": "Tue, 09 Oct 2018 01:00:00 GMT",
  "x-content-type-options": "nosniff",
  "etag": "W/\"6e-5ndzT6iGpj2E7RLnJjIh1jHCzW0\"",
  "x-download-options": "noopen",
  "x-frame-options": "DENY",
  "content-type": "application/json; charset=utf-8",
  "access-control-allow-origin": "http://18.222.75.237:3000",
  "access-control-allow-credentials": "true",
  "connection": "keep-alive",
  "vary": "Origin, Accept-Encoding",
  "content-length": "110",
  "x-xss-protection": "1; mode=block"
}
```

Example of JSON data

The API will call the `Init` chaincode in the fabric network and return the response to the browser.

Select a company using a post method to create an insuree. Enter this JSON request as follows:

```
{
  "$class": "com.packt.quickstart.claim.Init",
  "insureeId": "user-001",
  "firstName": "John",
  "lastName": "Smith",
  "ssn": "9999",
  "policyNumber": "string"
}
```

You should see a successful response, similar to the one shown in the following screenshot:

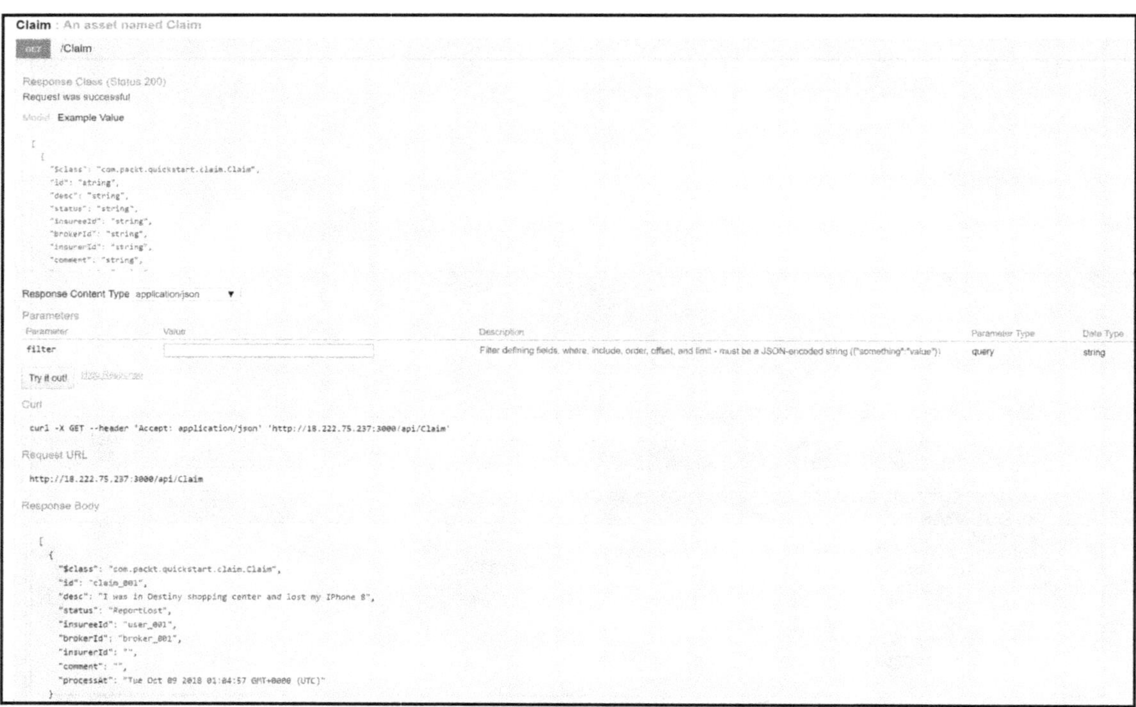

Selecting a company using a post method to create insuree, enter this JSON request

Select the `ReportLost Post` method from endpoints, provide the post JSON data, and click **Try it out!**:

```
{
  "$class": "com.packt.quickstart.claim.ReportLost",
  "claimId": "claim_001",
  "desc": "I was in Destiny shopping center and lost my IPhone 8",
  "insureeId": "user_001",
  "brokerId": "broker_001"
}
```

You should see a success response back from the blockchain.

To verify that the claim was successfully created in the network, you can select the claim get method and click **Try it out!** You should be able to get the claim result, as follows:

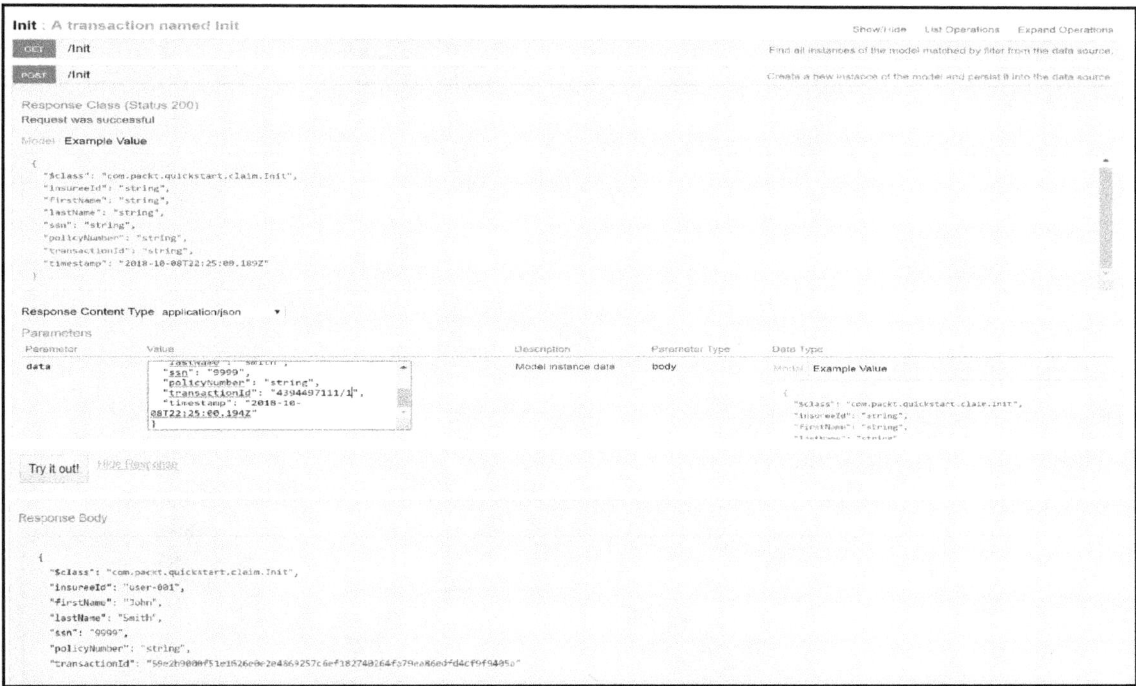

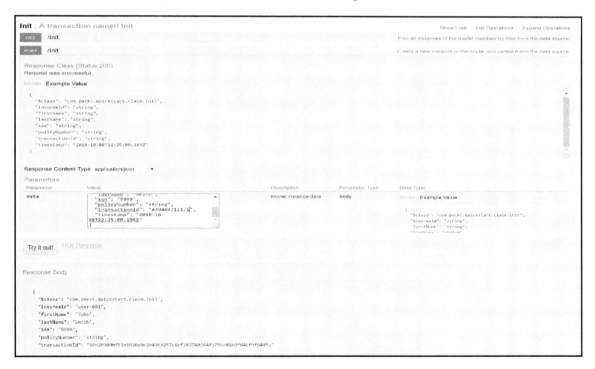

Verifying if the claim was sucessfully created in the network

Other insurance claims endpoint APIs will be quite similar to the ones we have explored.

Summary

We have reached the end of this chapter. In this chapter, we have overviewed Hyperledger Composer and installed the related tools. We used composer model language to develop the same insurance claim use case as in `Chapter 5`, *Exploring an Enterprise Blockchain Application Using Hyperledger Fabric*, and deployed it to the fabric network. Lastly, we integrated the application with a composer REST server to generate a client API and interacted with these APIs from the web.

At this point, you should be comfortable working with Hyperledger Composer. Now that we're at the end of this chapter, we have learned about the two most popular public and enterprise blockchains. As a blockchain developer, you should have the basic blockchain knowledge to be able to write your blockchain application. In the next chapter, we will discuss the various real world blockchain use cases.

7
Blockchain Use Cases

After completing the first six chapters, you should have sufficient knowledge to think about how to apply your newly acquired skills to resolving real-life problems. As discussed earlier, blockchain is considered to be a game-changing technology, which can potentially disrupt existing business models by making intermediary services obsolete and inspire the creation of new and cost-effective business models. However, this technology can not resolve all issues and its value can only be fully realized by combining it with other mature or emerging technologies, such as big data platforms, cloud computing, data science/AI, and IoT.

In this chapter, we first talk about popular blockchain use cases across industries, including financial, civil services, supply chain, IoT, and healthcare, at a high level. We will then proceed to a discussion of factors for consideration, before determining proper use cases and developing a successful DApp. Finally, we take the health data sharing use case and comment, at a high level, on building a DApp for it. Specifically, we cover the following topics:

- Examples of blockchain uses cases
- How to choose a proper use case
- In-depth discussion of the use case of healthcare data sharing

Blockchain use case examples

The evolution of technology has fundamentally changed people's lives. Throughout human history, machines have replaced humans for performing various tasks. For example, in agriculture, farming vehicles made farming work less labor-intensive and greatly increased productivity. In the US, as of 2008, less than 2 % of the population directly work in agriculture. They not only supply the food needed for the other 98% of the population, but also make the US the biggest agricultural products exporter. Examples in other areas include programmable telephone switchboards replacing telephone operators, and automatic elevators replacing elevator operators.

This trend of machines replacing humans sped up in the last several decades, largely due to the invention of computers. So far, there have been three computer-led revolutions in technology. Each of these revolutions fundamentally affected existing business models and inspired new ways of doing business. We are now at the dawn of the fourth phase: a blockchain technology-led revolution. The following are the phases:

- **Invention of mainframe and PC**: Computers replaced humans for performing repetitive computations faster and better. Applications of computers driving automation are numerous and everywhere.
- **Internet**: The internet refers to a globally interconnected network of computers. The arrival of the internet fundamentally changed the way services are delivered. For example, in the 90s, renting a video cassette or CD/DVD at a local rental store was a popular family entertainment activity on the weekends. Blockbuster was a household name offering rental services, and its business model worked well. In 2004, Blockbuster employed 84,300 people worldwide and had 9,094 stores in total. With the internet, new companies such as Netflix emerged and disrupted the reign of companies such as Blockbuster. Families no longer need to make a trip to a physical rental store to pick up a CD/DVD. Instead, they can downloaded a virtual copy of a movie from the internet. In 2010, Blockbuster filed for bankruptcy. Today, Netflix is a 145B company. The same story has repeated itself many times in other areas.
- **Social media sites**: Social media sites such as Facebook, Twitter, or YouTube not only changed existing business models, they changed the way people obtain news and how news is distributed. Papers and radio/TV-based news distribution are no longer the only channels for news dissemination. Many news publishers were forced to shut down due to the loss of subscribers. On the other hand, freelance news reporters started emerging via YouTube and so on. Social media sites have also fundamentally impacted governments as news censorship became more difficult.

Phase 4—blockchain technology: Even with social media sites, censorship—although more difficult—is still possible since information is hosted and processed at a centralized server, so censorship can be implemented at that centralized server. With a blockchain network, censorship is not practical thanks to the decentralized design of blockchain technology. The only way is to shut down all the nodes of the network within a country. The biggest impact of blockchain on existing business models comes from the fact that this technology will make intermediary services obsolete. It will particularly affect the financial industry, where most financial services are essentially intermediary. This technology is about to bring changes not just to the financial industry, but to virtually every other industry.

Next, we cite a few examples of potential blockchain technology applications. We use the word *potential*, since the technology is still evolving and its current form has many limitations. There is no guarantee that these use cases can be implemented. It will take a while before many of these use cases become a reality, and some may never come to fruition. Regardless of whether a use case can be implemented or not, we focus our discussions on business problems and on ideas of how business *pain points* can potentially be addressed via this technology. As the technology advances, for example with improvements in performance, some use cases will become a reality. We first talk about use cases in the financial industry.

Payment and settlement services

Reconciliation of transactions between banks is costly and time-consuming when performed traditionally. For example, in 2016, the US alone had 70B debit card transactions. In the same year, VisaNet (one of world's largest electronic payment networks) processed an average of 150 million transactions a day. With these high volumes, even a tiny saving in each transaction can lead to a huge reduction in the overall cost of doing business. In the case of stock trading, the complete cycle of a trade plus clearing and settlement take three days. A failure in reconciling a transaction could result in a significant monetary loss. (Therefore, a clearinghouse such as DTCC implements an insurance mechanism to mitigate settlement risks.) With blockchain technology, payment processing is increasingly moving towards instant payment worldwide. For example, Ripple can complete a cross-board payment in minutes. The technology combines transaction and settlement. It dramatically reduces the associated transaction costs. The steps of a transaction are visible to a requester. A recent research report claimed Ripple's payment cost is only 0.1% of the cost associated with a traditional transaction. Similarly, for stock trading, since a blockchain implementation merges trading and clearing/settlement into one action, there is no longer a settlement risk. An exchange member firm will not need to pay a premium for settlement insurance and will not require a large back office team dedicated to handling settlements. This will significantly reduce the cost of doing business for the firm.

Import and export finance

In goods trading, importers and exporters respectively use their banks for issuing **letter of credit** (**LC**) and settling payments. Blockchain will allow banks to simplify document management. It provides transparency to the parties involved and mitigates the potential risk of document fraud. It makes transaction reconciliation between and within financial institutions a lot simpler, leading to significant savings. The decentralized ledger provides auditable transaction logs, making legal disputes less likely and simpler to settle.

Immutable ledger

Book or record keeping methods, such as using a ledger, become increasingly complicated due to the increasing number of participants and the complexity of transactions. The traditional way of maintaining a ledger is for it to be centralized. This approach lacks transparency, leading to frequent disputes legally or not legally. It is also difficult to identify an error as parties involved in a transaction do not have an efficient real-time method to check and verify transaction facts against the ledger. Blockchain technology can resolve the issues seamlessly. The decentralized and immutable ledger maintained on the chain virtually eliminates any chance of a dispute and brings trust between parties in transactions. Blockchain allows for real-time queries and permits parties to ensure their correctness. Unlike the traditional way, where two trading parties kept entries in their respective ledgers, possibly leading to discrepancies, the blockchain ledger allows all parties to maintain a unified ledger, eliminating the possibility of inconsistencies.

Regulatory compliance and auditing

With its immutability, regulators can trust any information that they extract from transactions recorded on enterprise blockchains. Financial companies do not have to take steps to prepare data and invest heavily in implementing data governance to ensure the correctness of data. As a result, blockchain technology can potentially help lower the cost of regulatory compliance and auditing for financial companies in areas such as security trading, **anti-money laundering** (**AML**), and **know your customer** (**KYC**).

Identity theft detection

The decentralized blockchain system deters bank theft and hacking activities. The adoption of blockchain technology will make detection of identity theft easier. If a thief steals an identity and opens a bank account or makes a fraudulent tax claim, the affected individual can see all the accounts under his/her name and identify the suspicious activities. The person can then report them to a bank or the IRS immediately, preventing them from suffering further loss.

Funds back-office operation

Blockchain can be used to improve the efficiency of implementing measures to satisfy the regulation requirements of AML and KYC while onboarding a new client. It can help with funds' net present value calculation, as well as other back-office activities such as reconciliation and handling corporate actions (such as, stock splitting, company mergers and acquisitions, and so on).

Collateral management

In a traditional way, regardless of a bilateral or tri-party transaction, information on collateral is not available in real time to parties involved in a transaction. Blockchain can be used to provide a decentralized system for collateral management. It provides real-time transparency and maintains one copy of state on collateral usage, which removes the possibility of having inconsistent information on collateral due to parties keeping their individual records as well as a traditional collateral management approach.

In the previous section, we discussed examples of use cases for the financial industry. Next, we cover examples beyond the financial industry.

Healthcare systems

Blockchain can help to address the issue of lacking a way to manage health data efficiently. The adoption of blockchain technology can simplify medical data management. For example, a patient's medical history, diagnostic information, and test results are kept at their respective doctors' offices. Sharing medical information among doctors, for instance a patient's family physician and specialists, is time-consuming and difficult. This could lead to a delay in diagnosis or generatre redundant medical tests. The blockchain can make data sharing easier, while the confidential data is well protected. The detailed medical records can then be aggregated. The aggregated information can be made available to medical researchers, government agencies, and pharmaceutical or insurance companies. With simplification and worldwide access, health data sharing helps promote cooperation among researchers and pharmaceutical companies in the development of new treatments and drugs. Based on real health data, government agencies can make improved health policies. Medical insurance firms can utilize data to calculate the premiums for plans and reduce the cost of collecting the required data. The same goes for decentralizing the results of clinical trials. In summary, blockchain can revolutionize how health data is stored, managed, and shared. It will profoundly impact the development of the health industry as a whole.

Real estate trading and rental markets

In the US, realtors charge a broker fee, typically 5 to 6% of the selling price, for bringing a seller and a buyer together to make a real estate transaction. Lawyers charge hundreds of dollars for providing legal services to a buyer or seller. In New York city, a real estate broker typically charges a customer one month of rent, which is often thousands of USD, for facilitating a rental transaction. This is quite expensive compared to the limited services provided. Blockchain provides a much lower cost solution with the added value of providing transparency. A real estate blockchain network matches untrusted buyers/sellers or tenants/landlords for a deal. The scripted legal document, a smart contract, replaces mos legal services provided by a real estate lawyer, thus rendering them nonessential. No escrowsing accounts are required since blockchain combines transaction and settlement into one action. In other words, transferring ownership of a house and payment occur at the same time. A similar solution is applicable in the case of property rentals. This will lead to dramatic savings in transactions by both parties. Facing the threat posed by blockchain technology, realtors will either have to find an innovative way of providing value added services or change to a different occupation.

IP market

IP refers to intellectual property. This can be a digital or digitized asset such as a novel, a song, a movie, a painting, a patent, or a piece of software. Blockchain technology can potentially be used to set up a market for buying and selling IPs. This will allow an owner to sell an IP asset to a buyer. For example, upon completion of a novel, an author can generate a predetermined number of digital copies of the novel and sell directly to readers. Each digital copy has a pair of public/private keys and an address. Upon paying the price of the book, the title of this copy is transferred to a buyer. The buyer can in future resell the copy at a secondary IP market. This new business model does not involve a publisher. An author can pocket most of the proceeds from book sales.

Elections

The current way of conducting an election has multiple downsides. First, it often requires the physical presence of the person casting the vote. Many elections still rely on paper voting. This makes counting the result very time-consuming, labor-intensive, and expensive. It also may lead to a lengthy recount, which happened during the previous US presidential elections in several close-call states. The recounting took weeks or longer to complete. Manipulating the outcome, double voting, or faking a vote are other frequently cited problems, even during several highly watched elections in other countries.

Blockchain technology can be used to address these issues. With a blockchain-based election DApp, casting a vote can take place worldwide. Every voter is uniquely assigned an account, an address, making double voting infeasible. The result of an election is immutable. Therefore, manipulation of an election outcome is not possible. The technology brings another advantage by making worldwide, cross-border referendums feasible on issues such as environmental topics.

HR and recruiting

A common issue faced by the HR department at a large company is how to identify a candidate with the right skills, work experience, and educational background. Often, the solution is to hire a professional recruiter or headhunter, who either identifies candidates via personal networking or through scanning social media sites such as LinkedIn. The fee paid to a recruiter is equal to a month's salary for the hired candidate or more. Blockchain can be utilized to build a decentralized database of professionals. This can serve two purposes. First, it provides transparency to match employers and candidates. Second, every company can learn the history of a potential employee and the person's current employment status. This can help to filter out potential fraudsters getting employed by a company.

Public records

The government's civic administration office maintains different types of record, for example on citizens, tax returns, holders of deed and property titles, building permits, zoning information, patents, water pipeline and sewage layouts, and so on. They require continuous updates. In addition, these offices receive frequent inquiries. Keeping these records on paper is expensive since the government has to hire a team of office clerks to manage the records manually.Even in the case where records are electronically filed, hands are still needed to respond to inquiries. With a digital ledger hosted on a blockchain, inquiries can be met via software query tools instead of via an office clerk. This solution will safeguard the data from being altered for malicious purposes. This can help to reduce identity theft as well.

Reduce contract disputes

Blockchain is used internally by IBM for resolving contract disputes between partners on the network. According to IBM's estimates, an average of 0.9% of its 2.9 million transactions result in disputes. These disputes lead to around US $100 million in capital being tied, up and unable to be put to work to make a profit. The capital financing cost for $100 million is not trivial. There are also significant costs associated with resolving the disputes. With the blockchain solution, IBM can combine data provided by participants in the network and create a comprehensive view of all transactions. The blockchain provides strong privacy and confidentiality controls via an access-entitling governance mechanism. This solution has greatly reduced the number of disputes.

Sharing economy

Blockchain technology can be used to create a market to promote the sharing or rental of the residual value of an item or services to others. For example, one may have an underused computer that can be rented out to another user who needs a temporary boost in computational capacity. In this case, the blockchain sharing market can be used to complete such a rental arrangement. The platform essentially allows individuals to run a private rental business on virtually anything that is shareable. The blockchain technology-based market is suitable for any device whose usage can be conveniently shared digitally, such as a computer. The market can be used to facilitate the sharing of general services as well. For example, in a European country young people provide nursery services to elders in exchange for credits. The accumulated credits can be used to recieve similar services when a person becomes old. With the blockchain solution, the person will receive digital coins that may be called *ServiceCoin* for the services being provided to others and can spend the coins later to recieve a service. This can potentially be a solution to addressing the problem of the high cost of nursery care in the US.

Integration with IoT

IoT refers to Internet of Things. IoT is a network of many different types of things, such as physical devices, vehicles, home appliances, and sensors. These things are connected and can collect and share data. When combining blockchain technology and IoT, we can potentially implement many meaningful applications. They can have a lot of benefits such as providing convenience in people's lives, saving lives, and reducing the cost of conducting business. The following are a few possible use cases:

- A smart contract can be automatically called to place an order for additional laundry detergent when an embedded sensor detects the level of detergent is down the preset level.
- A health wristband or embedded sensor in clothing may detect vital statistics on a person pointing to the likelihood of a potential heart attack. It then automatically triggers a smart contract to send an order to a pharmacy store and an SMS or email alert to the person. When implemented well, this kind of application can save many lives.
- A built-in sensor in a refrigerator can detect the quantity of vegetables or meat and trigger a smart contract to order additional vegetables/meat from a local farmer and a meat supplier without the involvement of a grocery store. This will avoid costs added to grocery products by stores and lead to savings for consumers.
- When a hotel guest is ready to check out, the guest can simply drop a room key (or smart key) at a designated place. A sensor triggers a checkout smart contract. When triggered, the smart contract will access the data being collected via other sensors in the room, such as information on consumption of snacks/drinks at a mini-bar or possible damage to room facilities. Based on the collected data, the smart contract will calculate a final amount and complete the guest's checkout by invoking and completing a payment transaction. With such a solution, a guest does not need to visit the hotel reception desk and this saves the guest time. It also helps the hotel reduce operating costs since the hotel does not need to hire an employee to man the reception desk.

Facilitate commercial and social relationships

The Australian government entity, the **CSIRO** (**Commonwealth Scientific and Industrial Research**) Organisation , carried out scientific research for the benefit of Australia. The agency pointed out that the blockchain can be used as a database system that facilitates commercial and social relationships. An effective use of blockchain technology lies in complex markets with multiple organizations interacting with each other.

How to choose a proper use case

With so much speculation about blockchain technology and its potential impacts on existing business models, it is a time to be realistic. In Gartner's most recent *Hype Cycle for Emerging Technologies* report, blockchain is said to have entered the *trough of disillusionment* phase, the third phase of the company's *hype cycle* metric, as shown in the following screenshot:

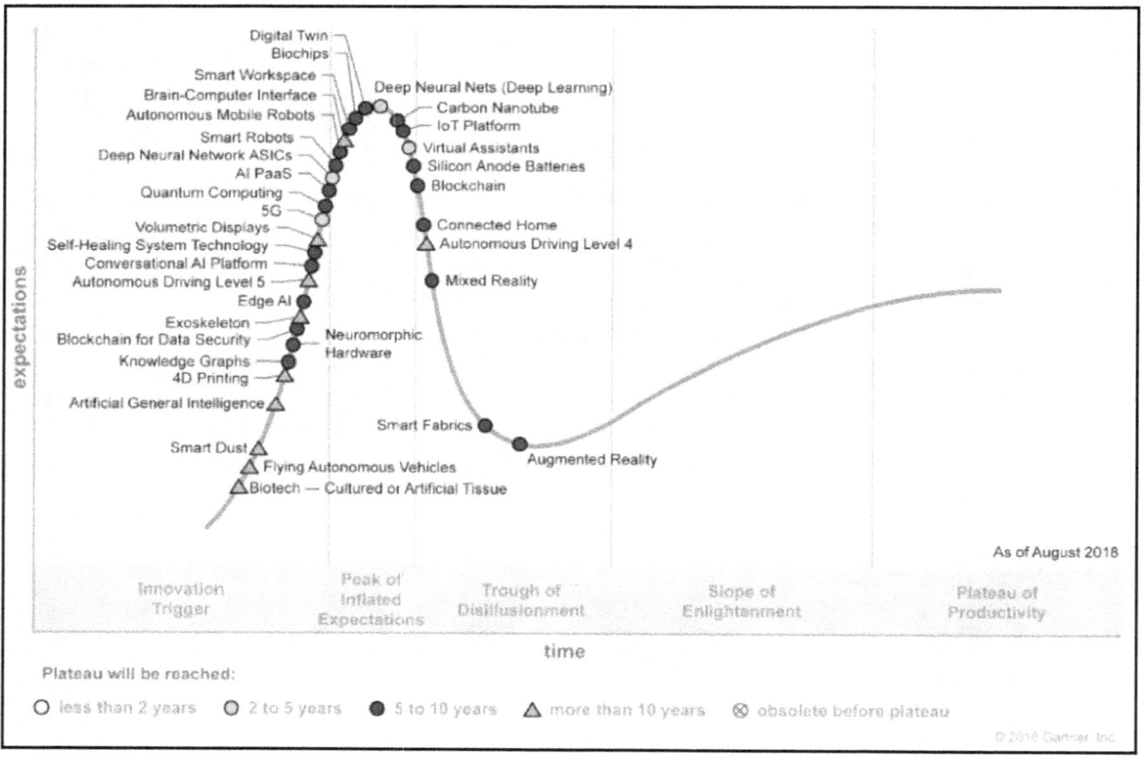

Between Q4 2017 and Q1 2018, the price of 1 BTC reached above 19K and then quickly dropped down 10k in a matter of days. It is 3.4K on December 11, 2018. This eye-popping roller-coaster in BTC price has led to the cooling down of frantic speculations on cryptocurrencies and consequently a reduction in investment in cryptocurrency projects. In addition, the limitations of the technology are also a factor, making the technology unsuitable for certain use cases. A well known issue is the low rate of **transactions per second** (**TPS**) inherited by most blockchain platforms from Bitcoin, as discussed in `Chapter 2`, *Ethereum Fundamentals*. Successful blockchain applications are still scarce and they are mainly concentrated in the financial industry. Ripple is a success story, which focuses on cash payments.

Since blockchain technology is not suitable for all use cases, it is important to choose a proper use case before jumping into action. The following comments can be useful to help you in determining which use case to work on and how to choose a blockchain platform for its implementation along with other architectural considerations:

- Not every use case is suitable for blockchain. For instance, many use cases can be implemented with traditional technology. It is true that blockchain is a data repository. If the sole purpose is to host data, choosing a regular database may be sufficient. Currently writing to a blockchain is still much slower than writing to a database. Insertion into a blockchain takes seconds or minutes. Insertion into a database takes only milliseconds. This makes databases a better choice in many use cases requiring high throughput, such as capturing credit/debit card transactions or equity trading market data. In the future, as performance and scalability improve, blockchain technology can be used for these use cases.
- In IoT use cases, an issue to consider is how to integrate an IoT device with a blockchain network. An IoT device is not a computer. As a result, an IoT device cannot be a node of the blockchain network. One possible solution is to link the device with a node on the network via APIs. The node interacts with the blockchain ledger and triggers the corresponding smart contracts upon receiving a signal from the IoT device. Performance is also an issue. Some IoT devices, such as airplane sensors, generate high-frequency measurements. A low TPS blockchain network cannot respond quickly to requests from these devices.

- The block size of a blockchain platform is limited. For example, Bitcoin has a block size restricted to around 1 MB. The following graph (from `blockchain.com`) shows its average block size history up to October 2018. For use cases such as an IP market for selling a novel or a movie, detailed information on a digital asset requires a lot of storage space. One can consider an architectural design of combining on-and off-chain storage to resolve the limited block size issue. Details about a digital asset can be saved off-chain at a centralized location. Ethereum has already adopted the on-and off-chain data storage approach:

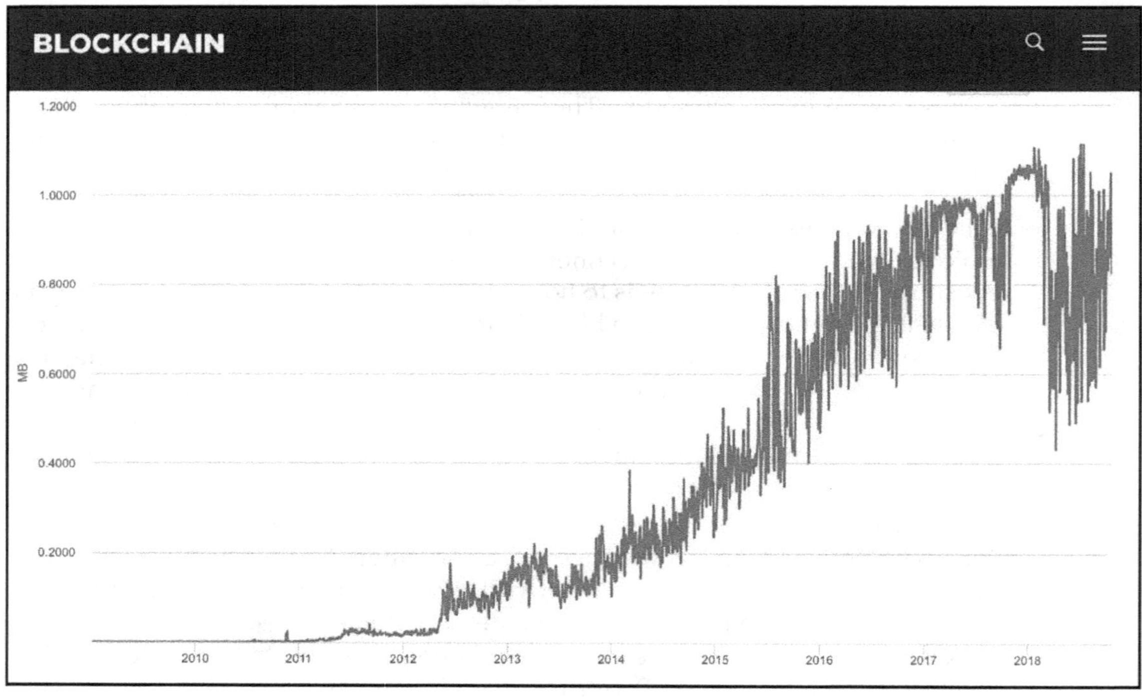

- If a use case involves a digitized asset, a few issues need to be addressed for managing the underlying physical assets:
    - The physical asset needs to be notarized in order to prove its authenticity.
    - A solution is needed to ensure that the underlying asset remains the same and is not changed between the time it is notarized andwhen it is transferred in its title.
    - Similar to the digital coin double spending issue, a solution is needed to ensure that a physical asset is mapped to one and only one digital asset.

  - Valuable physical assets require secured places for storage. When ownership is transferred digitally, the corresponding ownership on the underlying asset needs to be recorded and transferred. A possible solution could be borrowed from bullion (gold) trading. The physical gold can be stored at a safe place, like the NY Fed gold vault. When a pile of gold bars changes ownership, the physical gold bars do not leave the vault.
- Although Ethereum is a generic platform supporting DApp development, its implementation involves a digital coin. Whenever a cryptocurrency is part of a solution, one may need to deal with legal complications associated with it. For example, in the US, BTC is defined as an asset, not a currency. In other words, there is a tax implication (for instance, sales tax) when a BTC is sold to a buyer. Certain countries such as China prohibit cryptocurrency trading. As a result, an enterprise blockchain solution such as **Hyperledger Fabric** (**HF**) may be preferred since its implementation does not involve a cryptocurrency.
- Many use cases such as healthcare data sharing or credit data digitization are not suitable for public use. A permission-based enterprise (or private) blockchain is needed instead of a public blockchain such as Ethereum.
- Another advantage of a private chain such as HF or R3's Corda over Ethereum is that both HF and Corda support development in Java, while Ethereum requires a programmer to learn a new language such as Solidity. Given the scarcity of talent in Solidity, it is difficult and expensive to find qualified developers. On the other hand, turning a Java programmer into a HF or Corda developer could be an easier solution.
- Blockchain technology implies the guaranteed execution of a scripted legal document, a smart contract, which makes untrusting parties feel comfortable doing transactions. If a use case does not require a guaranteed transaction, then it is not a suitable use case. For instance, blockchain is not needed to replace the traditional internet dating site. Dating is very personal and it does not lead to a guaranteed transaction—a marriage.
- If blockchain is only used for the purpose of being a distributed ledger, it is not justifiable due to the cost associated with a blockchain solution. If fault tolerance and providing transparency are the primary goals, a distributed ledger can be implemented in a traditional way by making identical copies of the ledger at multiple nodes without the need to involve additional components, such as Bitcoin's mining and consensus mechanism. The consensus component was introduced to resolve the double spending issue. A distributed ledger does not involve double spending. In other words, blockchain is overkill if one only needs a distributed ledger.

- Blockchain currently is still not a suitable solution for many use cases requiring high throughput, such as stock trading or credit card transactions. Existing blockchain platforms are many magnitudes slower than other platforms (for instance, traditional databases) for hosting transaction data. For example, a specialized database, KDB, is needed to save market data in terms of billions of records a day.
- Since smart contracts are scripted legal documents, there are legal challenges to be dealt with:
  - Are local laws applicable when a smart contract runs? If the answer is yes, how do you deal with conflicts with local laws, a scenario when the contract is legal at some locations of nodes and not at other locations of nodes?
  - Regulations and laws are not fully developed on blockchain and cryptocurrency. A US lawmaker recently pushed the IRS to clarify regulations on blockchain.
  - Since the execution of a smart contract is automatic and unstoppable, a blockchain application could be ruled to be unlawful when it cannot sufficiently address illegal activities such as money laundering.
  - Cryptocurrency receives different statuses in different countries. For example, in the US it is defined as an asset and in Singapore, it is considered to be a currency.

DApp use case – healthcare data sharing

In this subsection, we look at one use case in more detail and talk about steps leading to the implementation of a DApp. The use case of healthcare data sharing will be examined further. Here, only ideas are discussed, which are not necessarily implementable. Most of the discussions focus on business and architectural considerations.

The business problem

Before getting to implementing a DApp, one should start with the business problem by asking questions such as *What are the challenges or the pain points*? In the case of healthcare data, examples of challenges are as follows:

- **Digitization**: Many patients' medical records are available only on paper. This is particularly true for family physician offices, which are usually small. When a patient visits a physician's office, it is still a common scene for a doctor's office receptionist to search the file cabinets and pull out a folder with the patient's medical history. The records are then handed over to the physician. The physician reads the records while talking to the patient. This approach is not scalable and risky. A natural disaster such as flooding or fire can easily destroy these records. When a patient changes physician, the old records are not transferred. The new physician's office will set up a new folder and start to accumulate the medical history for the patient. Due to the loss of old records, some medical tests may need to be redone, resulting in additional costs and inconvenience to the patient. More importantly, the loss of history could lead to losing precious time that could be used for curing a disease.
- **Timeliness**: Since a patient's medical records are physically maintained at multiple offices, sharing the records, for example between the patient's family physician and a specialist, is difficult and time-consuming. To facilitate sharing the records, the patient first gives his/her physician's contact information to the specialist's office. Then, a specialist's office receptionist contacts the physician's office. The physician's office makes an arrangement to send the information via fax or regular mail. This approach is slow, expensive, and insecure. A patient's medical information can potentially be seen by unauthorized parties during the information transfer and the stolen insurance information can be used for malicious purposes.
- **Ownership**: Medical records are the health history of a patient. The patient should be the owner of the medical data. A doctor's office is merely the custodian. In reality, this is rarely the case. Whoever maintains the medical records becomes the de facto owner and makes decisions on how the data is used or accessed.
- **Transparency**: Since medical records are on paper and scattered at doctors' offices, individual and institutional users such as medical researchers, government agencies, and insurance companies do not have a convenient way to access aggregated medical information for legislative and other purposes. Access to the aggregated medical information, which does not involve confidential information about individuals, can be beneficial for the advancement of medical research, prioritizing medicine development, or making government health policies.

A blockchain solution

After identifying a business problem and its *pain points*, the next step is to search for a proper solution. For the previous business problem, a general solution is needed to build a computer-based healthcare data sharing platform. The platform will allow authorized parties such as doctors, researchers, government agencies, insurance companies, and pharmaceutical firms to access the medical data. Developing such a platform requires a tremendous amount of work. Digitization of existing paper records alone is well beyond our capability and requires the involvement of many groups and organizations. Since this book focuses on blockchain technology, we will concentrate on the blockchain part of a solution without worrying too much about the feasibility of its actual implementation.

Blockchain technology combined with other technologies, such as big data platforms and data science, is proposed. The blockchain will be used for hosting transactions. The big data platform provides sufficient space for hosting the bulk of the healthcare data at the detailed and aggregation levels. The data science-based analytics component computes the aggregated medical data and derives the analytical summaries.

- **Data repository**: The size of patient healthcare data can easily be in terabytes. It is not feasible to host healthcare data on-chain only. It is logical to choose the approach of combining on- and off-chain records for saving detailed medical data. In fact, the Ethereum blockchain has already used the idea of maintaining state variables off-chain, while having transactions and smart contracts saved on the chain. The body of a patient's medical information can be saved off-chain and its hash is saved on the chain. The hash is used here to prevent medical records from being modified without authorization. Each patient's medical record will be assigned with an address. When a patient's medical record is updated, a transaction with the type *update* is generated on chain. A new hash corresponding to the updated medical records of a patient is generated and saved on the chain. The updated records will have a new address. Similarly, when a user accesses a patient's medical records, a transaction with the type *access* is saved on chain. The digital assets of these transactions are the medical records.

- **Choice of blockchain platform**: Choosing a proper blockchain platform is an important architectural decision. There are technical and non-technical factors to be considered. One key non-technical consideration is the legal implication if a DApp solution involves a cryptocurrency, as different countries have different laws on cryptocurrency trading. Trying to work out a coin-based DApp following these laws is a daunting task and is not worth the effort. The purpose of our DApp is to resolve a business problem, not to issue a digital coin. A generic public blockchain platform such as Ethereum involves a digital coin or token. An enterprise blockchain platform such as Hyperledger Fabric does not involves a cryptocurrency. Therefore, HF should be considered. Since HF is permission-based, its consensus algorithm does not require heavy and lengthy computations. Therefore, HF provides a higher TPS. It also contains an access entitlement and control component, which is required for managing medical information access.
- **Analytics component**: An analytical component is needed to perform tasks such as aggregating detailed medical information and providing useful statistics. The aggregation is mandatory in order to mask confidential individual information and make the medical information usable by users such as medical researchers, government agencies, or insurance/pharmaceutical companies. A patient's detailed medical information should only be used by the patient's doctor with the patient's permission. The aggregated data should, as a minimum, make it impossible to reverse-engineer the information for any patient.
- **Data protection**: With any DApp implementation, protecting digital assets hosted on the platform is a key requirement. There are many examples of hackers attacking blockchain platforms, cryptocurrency exchanges, or wallets and stealing millions of USD in digital coins. Some well known incidents are Mt Gox and Bitfinex being hacked a few years ago. Attaching on Zaif is a more recent example. In addition, protection of a patient's privacy is legally required. Failure to comply with privacy laws will lead to the shutdown of a DApp application and result in costly legal suits. To protect a patient's medical information, we can encrypt off-chain data. When a patient grants permission to a doctor to access medical records, a temporary key will be provided. The doctor's office uses the temporary key to obtain a masked private key for decrypting the records. The private key should not be visible to the doctor's office afterward. Only the temporary key is visible and is valid for a short period of time. A new temporary key will be generated for the next access request. The aggregated information may not need to be encrypted. However, access to the information is strictly controlled based on a well defined authentication and entitlement model.

- **Backend component**: The backend component refers to smart contract development. Multiple contracts are needed to provide rules governing transactions, including uploading medical records, accessing detailed medical records, or querying the aggregated data. Since these transactions are on the chain, they provide an auditing trail of data being uploaded and how data is accessed. With these audit trails, a patient can easily monitor his/her medical information use and effectively protect his/her privacy and personal health information.
- **Frontend component**: To complete a DApp, a frontend component is needed. This component includes interfaces with users and interactions with the HF ledger or the analytics component. Interfaces with users allow a user such as a doctor's office receptionist to upload or update medical records. It also contains GUI tools for users to access both detailed and aggregated medical information. Any request to access medical information is first passed to an authorization verification module. After the request passes the permission check, it is then sent to the modules, which interact with a HF node to trigger the corresponding smart contracts and execute the request. These modules also interact with the blockchain network for data uploads.

The following chart displays how users interact with health data sharing platform components:

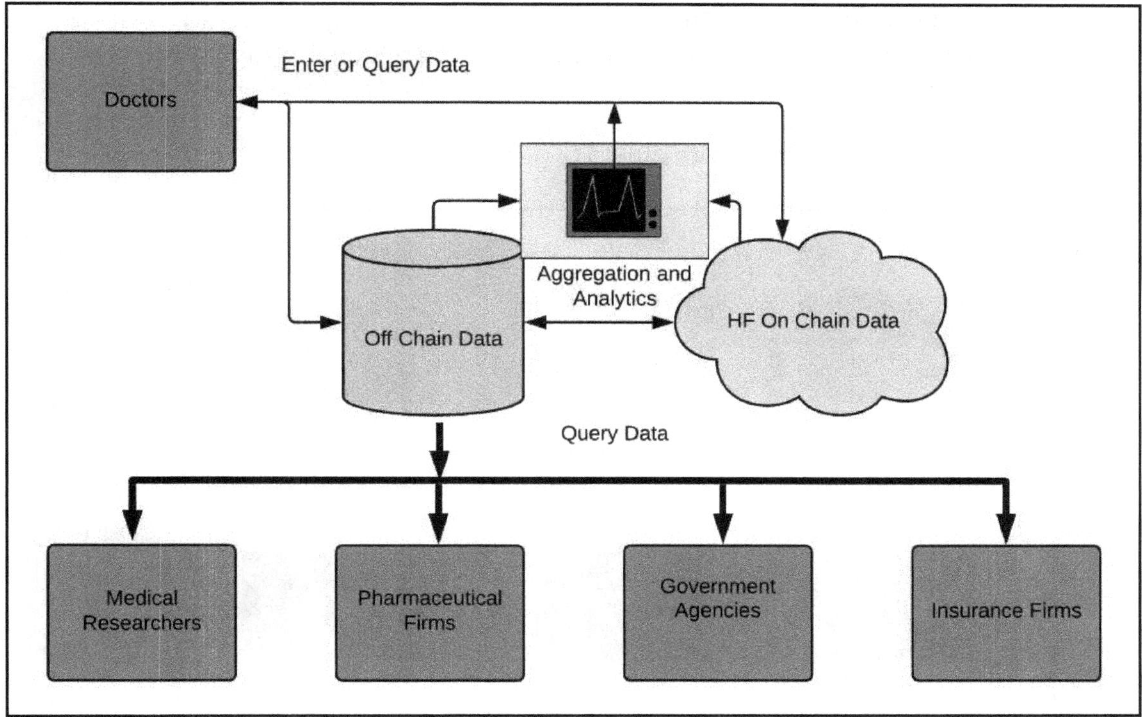

Users interaction with the health data sharing platform's components

The implementation of both frontend and backend components requires in-depth knowledge of blockchain and GUI development. IDE preparation and setup alone are not an easy task. Several startups step in to fill in the gaps and make these tasks easier. With these tools, a user no longer needs to write code to perform repetitive tasks such as environment setup, testing, and deployment. Instead, the user simply clicks on a few buttons. As a result, developers can focus on resolving a real business problem.

- **Parties involved**: The platform involves several parties. Doctor's offices are the primary data uploaders, as well as the users of the patient's detailed medical records. Medical researchers, government agencies, pharmaceutical companies, and insurance companies are users of the aggregated medical information.

- **Architectural diagram**: The following architectural diagram shows a layered design for implementing the healthcare data sharing platform. The top layer contains the frontend components. The middle layer is for off-chain data processing and analytics. The bottom layer is for backend components containing smart contracts, along with other HF components:

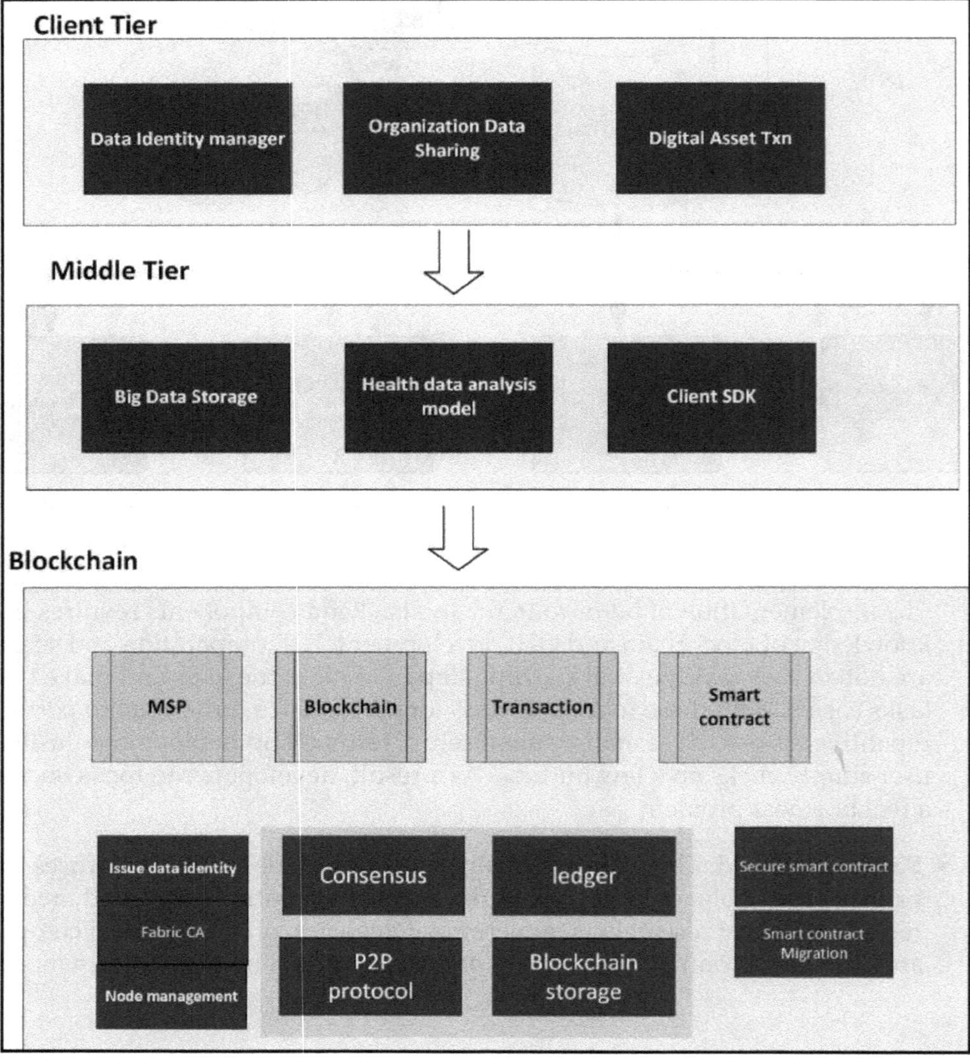

- **Project funding**: Sufficient funds need to be raised to support the healthcare data sharing project. One idea is to set up a blockchain startup and lobby potential investors to fund efforts. Nowadays, setting up and running a startup are much easier thanks to emerging technologies and online services. For example, cloud computing vendors such as Linode provide the affordable hardware supplies needed by a startup. Similarly, by utilizing WeChat members of a startup can have visual meetings worldwide without incurring any cost. Google Drive, Slides, Docs, and Sheets can serve as a virtual team's document collaboration and sharing software. GitHub is for software sharing and version control. For financial auditing, firms such as BitAudit (`http://www.bitaudit.vip/`) specialize in providing auditing services for blockchain technology firms. This is helpful given the fact that laws on cryptocurrency and blockchain technology have not matured yet and are still evolving.

Summary

As was the case for the internet in the nineties, blockchain is at the dawn of the Blockchain age. This technology will disrupt existing business models and give birth to new models. It will inspire the emergence of community economies built on a blockchain network, where every participant makes contributions to, and receives benefits from, the community. There is no longer a single entity that controls and receives dividends from the economy.

In this chapter, we have discussed use cases across industries to give you a flavor of potential blockchain applications. Given the limitations of the existing technology, not all these cases can be immediately implemented. As the technology progresses, more use cases can be tackled. Finally, we talked about important factors to be considered in selecting a proper use case and the steps to be followed in developing a complete DApp through an in-depth discussion on the healthcare data sharing use case.

Other Books You May Enjoy

If you enjoyed this book, you may be interested in these other books by Packt:

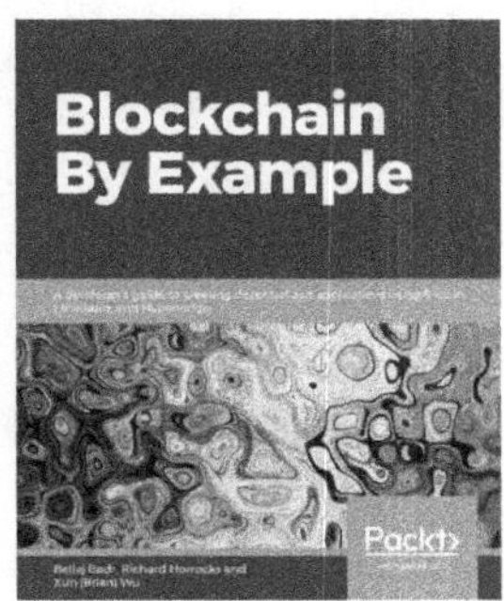

Blockchain By Example
Bellaj Badr, Xun (Brian) Wu

ISBN: 9781788475686

- Grasp decentralized technology fundamentals to master blockchain principles
- Build blockchain projects on Bitcoin, Ethereum, and Hyperledger
- Create your currency and a payment application using Bitcoin
- Implement decentralized apps and supply chain systems using Hyperledger
- Write smart contracts, run your ICO, and build a Tontine decentralized app using Ethereum
- Implement distributed file management with blockchain
- Integrate blockchain into existing systems in your organization

Blockchain for Enterprise
Narayan Prusty

ISBN: 9781788479745

- Learn how to set up Raft/IBFT Quorum networks
- Implement Quorum's privacy and security features
- Write, compile, and deploy smart contracts
- Learn to interact with Quorum using the web3.js JavaScript library
- Learn how to execute atomic swaps between different networks
- Build a secured Blockchain-as-a-Service for efficient business processes
- Achieve data privacy in blockchains using proxy re-encryption

Leave a review - let other readers know what you think

Please share your thoughts on this book with others by leaving a review on the site that you bought it from. If you purchased the book from Amazon, please leave us an honest review on this book's Amazon page. This is vital so that other potential readers can see and use your unbiased opinion to make purchasing decisions, we can understand what our customers think about our products, and our authors can see your feedback on the title that they have worked with Packt to create. It will only take a few minutes of your time, but is valuable to other potential customers, our authors, and Packt. Thank you!

Index

C

www.ingramcontent.com/pod-product-compliance
Lightning Source LLC
Chambersburg PA
CBHW080524060326
40690CB00022B/5021

* 9 7 8 1 7 8 9 8 0 7 9 7 4 *